Inner Journeys

Explorations of the Soul

Inner Journeys

Explorations of the Soul

Dr. G. Michael Vasey

THOTH PUBLICATIONS
Loughborough, Leicestershire

First Edition 2005

Copyright © 2005 Dr. G Michael Vasey

A CIP catalogue record for this book is available from the
British Library.
Cover design by Allison Gill

ISBN 1 870450 81 7

Printed and bound in Great Britain

Published by Thoth Publications
64, Leopold Street, Loughborough, LE11 5DN
web address: www.thoth.co.uk
email: enquiries@thoth.co.uk

Contents

For Paul, Liam and Jon

Acknowledgements

For my wife, Maureen, to prove to you that all those hours of reading and candle burning were worthwhile – although you already knew that. To my children for teaching me about the nature of true love and self sacrifice. To my parents, an explanation for the traumas we witnessed together and for supporting a demanding child.

Particular thanks and love to Elizabeth Anderton Fox, my SOL Supervisor, who has spent many hours reading my meditation diary and responding to my questions with patience and love. Thanks also to Dolores Ashcroft-Nowicki, for her help with this project, particularly her foreword, and her husband Michael Nowicki, for providing the structure and content of the SOL course and sending out my lessons in a timely fashion. Finally, thanks to the late John Fox for pointing to the SOL in the first place.

Foreword

When one enters a school for spiritual training there will always be a time of apprehension. What will it be like, what will I be asked to do, will I be able to cope? In actual fact 90% of students find all their questions answered within a few weeks and settle down to their studies with varying degrees of enthusiasm punctuated by the odd moments of boredom. Studying the occult is like any other study, you have good and bad days, some parts are interesting and others make you want to throw your papers out of the window.

But until now there have been few people who have actually sat down to write about their experiences, their hopes, fears, visions and disappointments while undertaking such a course. That is why this book is so important for both SOL students and those working in any spiritual school or Order.

The writer is a man whose life from an early age has been inexorably drawn towards spiritual study. Throughout the book you share with him the early days of family life and college and his struggle to pinpoint and control the psychic talents within him. He takes the reader through all his trials and tribulations, the highs and lows of his search, the training he eventually undertakes, and the way in which he finally found his path.

For those beginning the SOL or any spiritual course, read this before you start. It pulls no punches, it tells you frankly that you will find it often tedious and boring, but you will also find it at other times uplifting and exhilarating.

Those with no real insight have the idea that in ancient times every temple student lived a life of exciting ritual alternating with divine visionary experiences. In point of fact their lives were very like ours, full of humdrum tasks lightened by the relatively few exciting bits. A study of the occult is still like that and this book makes that clear. It is honest, down to earth, and very practical, and this makes it a valuable tool for those following in Michael's footsteps as he makes his way towards his goal.

I recommend it to all SOL people past, present and future. This is what you can expect from the course, and from your training. The author has my vote of confidence and thanks for an important addition to the SOL reading list.

Dolores Ashcroft-Nowicki
Director of Studies SOL

Fool's Journey

If you need some answers
Look deep inside your mind
For the inside is the outside
Where all answers you can find

On the Fool's long journey
You must start right at the end
And walk your way backwards
Imagination - just pretend

Carrying life's baggage
Walking on the edge of doom
Where the Sun is new and hot
And smiles back at the Moon

The Emperor sits on his throne
But the Empress bears a sign
Parents to all creation
Through all of endless time

The Devil speaks of bondage
You must die to be newborn
Learn the answer to the riddle
Set before the primal dawn

Cast a stone into your mind pool
And watch it ripple through
For the answer to your question
Will be found deep within you

When travelling this journey
You must learn to be the Fool
And look for words of wisdom
In the humble Mason's tool

For in the Understanding
Of Knowledge lies the key
The Fool was once the prodigal
And I know that Fool is me!

Chapter One

FIRST STIRRINGS

Over the centuries, the occult and magick have been misunderstood by the public. This perception is based, in my view, on a mistaken understanding of what "the occult" really is. Partly, these misperceptions are based on a Hollywood-type portrayal of the occult or that of paperback horror books, and partly, they are based on various religious assessments of what the occult is. The term 'Magick,' of course, invokes similar views. As a result, many people recoil in horror at the very idea of studying the occult or magick, but I believe they do so without understanding the truth of the matter or because of a taught bias that has little to do with the reality of the practice of the occult. If nothing else, I hope that this book will begin to re-establish the balance between the reality and these misperceptions.

The word "occult" simply means "hidden". The success of novels about wizards and schools of wizardry in particular has brought the concept of magick, and hence the occult, to the fore in modern western society. The success of these and similar books demonstrates the deep yearning in society for a more magickal life. The growing interest in all forms of the occult from astrology to witchcraft is deeply linked to the beginnings of a subconscious desire to re-awaken from the materialism of life today. However, pursuit of an occult path is not what one might expect and it is certainly not the sinister darkness that some people would have you believe.

For me, the occult, or Magick, is a journey deep into the core of my being. It is a voyage of inner discovery that at times, sweeps away my own long-held points of view and shakes the foundations on which I exist. It is a psychological exploration of me and my world and it is performed using powerful and ancient symbols and techniques proven to be successful through the ages.

It has been said that the occult journey is not for everyone. Much about the occult is left unspoken or hidden in allegory. The intent behind the mysteriousness that surrounds study of occult methods and thinking is not elitism nor indeed is it an attempt to hide some deep dark secret. It is simply based on the understanding that unleashing the inner forces is to be done carefully, slowly and patiently. Because occult study is fundamentally an exploration of the self performed using ancient symbols, glyphs and methods.

Against this background, I started on an occult path five years ago. I was the Fool seeking answers but I wasn't sure what it was that I was looking for. Why then did I choose this particular direction for answers? There are many things one can do during life for entertainment, or to learn and to explore. Perhaps it was because from the earliest age I can recall and, according to my parents, from even before that, I had perceived things that others did not. Although these perceptions had often terrified me to the core, it was simply time to find out what this was all about and why I was so afraid.

So, in 1999, after conducting some online research, I applied to study with an organisation within the UK called the Servants of the Light (SOL)[1]. A real school of occult science, the organization is run on a shoestring budget and, the incredible energy of Dolores Ashcroft-Nowicki and a small number of school graduates that voluntarily mentor, guide and supervise its 6000 students around the world. Taking a programme of 50 lessons at a pace of one about every month by correspondence, I embarked on a life changing journey - one that I wish to share with others. However, I do want to be absolutely clear that this book is about my own experiences and that it does not purport in any way to reflect the aims, teaching or objectives of the SOL.

---

[1] The Servants of the Light school website may be found at www.servantsofthelight.org

Chapter Two

WHAT THE STARS MADE ME

As I look back, I have lived much of my life at the constant beck and call of one thing, one emotion – fear. It's amazing the things that we do to avoid situations and events that make us feel uncomfortable, never mind those that invoke fear. And fear in some form or other has been at the root of my personality for much of my life.

For example, for many years I avoided flying because it terrified me. For months before a scheduled flight, I obsessed irrationally over my fear of boarding the flight; waking up each night for weeks before with palpitations and cold clammy palms. I found myself imagining the worst and yet I also spent many hours with my son watching planes take off and land at the local airport. It was an obsession with my fear of flying.

When I think of all of the places, people and events that I missed or did not experience simply because I was afraid to fly! In fact, when you really analyse what drives and motivates you as a person there is a good chance that, if you are honest, you will find that it is also some sort of fear. It might be fear of rejection or of being left out. It may be fear of being ignored but most importantly, it may be fear of failure.

Throughout my life I have done things, said things, and believed things simply to avoid circumstances that I was afraid to confront. In essence, I have been the perfect example of a person that avoids anything that makes me afraid or indeed, might make me afraid. Every act, every decision, and even many of my thoughts have been governed by fear and worry. So it should be no surprise that many who knew me might describe me as an unfriendly so and so! It's not that I am a bad person. After all I have never been in trouble with the law, I do have good friends, lots of colleagues, and a family that loves and respects me, but I made it hard for them all the same.

The eldest of three sons, I grew up in Hull, Yorkshire. Middle working class, my parents both worked hard to give my brothers and I the very best life possible. We had two holidays a year, often abroad, and weekends away in the caravan. I was given every opportunity to succeed and indeed I was the first and, to date, only member of our family ever to attend college.

However, perhaps by virtue of being born an Aquarian, there was always something different about me. I saw, heard and sensed things that others apparently did not. A little like the child in the movie 'The Sixth Sense', this caused me to be very afraid, both of what I experienced, and of sharing those experiences with others. Even at the earliest age, I would bring my parents running to my bedroom with my screams and then explain in all sincerity that a little blue man had jumped out of my mirror and then made faces at me! Fortunately, my father shared my extrasensory perception and was both willing and able to believe me.

The first experience that I recall was lying in bed one night and sensing the atmosphere slowly grow cold and tense. Opposite me, my brother, with whom I then shared a room, lay in his bed sleeping but I dare not even whisper to him. Something was not right. Slowly, I sat up to see a grayish, wispy, but plainly visible figure of a Cavalier complete with broad brimmed hat and sword in my bedroom. Sitting at an invisible desk, the man was feverishly writing with his quill and ink when he suddenly got up, walked with purpose across the room and out through the wall. I screamed.

Similar and constant occurrences caused me to sleep with the lights on and completely under my bedclothes for years. Strangely enough, several years later, I found out that the house was actually built on the grounds of an estate dating back to the 1600s and so perhaps, a Cavalier in my bedroom was not so strange after all.

My first lesson on the consequences of openly talking about the occult was when I was barely a teenager. With many strange experiences already behind me, I developed an obsession with reading any books that I could find in the local library about ghosts, psychic phenomena, and spiritualism. Both fascinated and curious, I read these books avidly but then realized that I had scared myself to the point where sleep was useless! At about that time, our Religious Education teacher at school was encouraging his students to get up in front of the class and discuss various topics of relevance. I chose to get up and tell my classmates about the occult and spiritualism, and ended up taking an entire 60 minute class with an enrapt audience. All the while thinking that my class mates were interested in the topic and naturally amazed at my knowledge of it, I soon found out that they were actually sat speechless in awe at what a freak I was! Never again did I ever mention anything to do with the occult through all my school days. But there it is again. Fear as a motivator. I was different, I had experiences and interest different from those considered the norm and, as a result, my own friends were afraid of me.

Nevertheless, I continued to read and seek out knowledge on the subject wherever I could find it. For a while I attended meetings of a group of people belonging to the Church for Spiritual and Psychic Research that met weekly at a local Methodist Church. Looking back, it probably was rather strange to have a twelve or thirteen year old attending meetings with a group of people whose average age was in their mid-fifties. However, they were kind enough to include me after obtaining the necessary permission from my parents and they provided me with access to a very nice library of books and I read them avidly.

During my teenage years, all hell broke loose. Perhaps this was as much about hormones as anything else, but our house seemed to progressively develop an unpleasant presence that made itself felt far too often. There would be thumping, bangs and crashes from the loft, sighs and moans when I least expected them, and worse still - footsteps. Doors opened for no apparent reason and things moved around the house at will. It was like having an outbreak of poltergeist activity.

For example, one evening in my late teens I came home from the pub just drunk enough to feel that I could get some sleep. I was visiting for the weekend from College and I always needed to have a couple of beers before I could sleep in that house. I was sleeping on the floor of my brother's room and he was already soundly asleep when I lay down or rather passed out. Despite my drunken condition, I was suddenly aware of the front door of the house being opened. It's amazing how alert you become when you are scared half to death. I was no longer feeling that warm woozy effect of alcohol but was now sat bolt upright, the hairs on my body stiff with fear.

"I did lock the door didn't I?" I said to myself trying to recall if I had checked the lock as I had stumbled through the doorway. I knew I had. Next, I heard a quiet low pitch moaning and groaning that sent chills running up my spine. It was so quiet that I could hear the silence as a continual buzz only occasionally punctuated by the low moans. Then, I heard footsteps coming slowly up the staircase as if the person on the stairs was struggling to climb each step. As this was happening, my heart was racing and the noisy silence was now drowned out by the sound of my own pounding heartbeat deep inside my bursting chest. When finally, I realized that whatever or whoever this was had now reached the landing, I found that I could actually move and started to back away from the bedroom door slowly and as soundlessly as possible. As I did so, the door started to slowly open and I let out a scream that was loud enough to wake the entire city of Hull. Strangely enough, only moments later, my father burst through the door with such an angry look on his face that I thought he was about to chastise me for screaming. Instead, he simply asked if I was OK and told me that he too had heard our intruder.

Whatever this phenomenon was, it occurred more and more often and with greater observable physical activity as time went on. One evening, sitting with a girl friend in our living room in the early hours of a Saturday morning, a similar event occurred and the sight of a door opening by itself was enough to send her home for the evening. At least it wasn't just my imagination!

My father has told me on a few occasions that his mother, who died before I was born, was a Medium. He has also spent a lifetime being fearful of seeing and hearing things that others did not. His fear of these phenomena came from an incident that occurred to him as a small child. His mother had told my father and his brother that she wanted to introduce them to her 'guide' and, according to my Father, she actually began to change facially to a small Chinese man in front of them. Plainly, neither he nor his small brother was encouraged by this excellent exhibition of mediumship. Despite that, I have often wished that I could talk to his mother and have her help me, and him.

At college it seemed that I was finally free of this shadow and I began to believe that our home was simply haunted or perhaps subject to some sort of poltergeist activity that held me at its centre. However, it was not to be. Only weeks into my college days, as I made my way from the Students' Union building to my accommodation on the 19th floor of a campus building, I noticed a suspicious looking character that appeared to be following me rather furtively. As I entered the elevator, he followed me in peering sideways at me and looking away whenever I caught his eye. As the lift arrived at my floor, I was hoping it was just my imagination and perhaps he would continue up to the top floor above me. But, as I left the lift, he followed and as I reached the doorway into the set of six study bedrooms, shared kitchen, and bath that was my home, he was still right there behind me.

"Do you want something?" I asked looking at him accusingly.

"Gary, I want to talk to you," he said quietly.

"How do you know my name?" I asked in surprise.

"I know a lot about you." he replied. "And I must speak with you – Now if possible."

Reluctantly, I let him in to my study bedroom and he introduced himself as an Indonesian student. He practiced meditation, he said, and he had been asked by his guide to talk to me and help with some challenges that I was facing.

Anantha and I actually became firm friends from that point forward. He knew an awful lot about me for someone I had just met and that seemed both mysterious and alluring. He tried to help me understand that I was sensitive and that this sensitivity meant that I was open to the flotsam and jetsam of the astral world. He also told me that my uncontrolled reaction – pure fear – was attracting things that I was better off without and he started to teach me some psychic self defence methods. While useful, the problem was that at the smallest hint of any phenomenon, I became a total wreck and fear possessed me completely.

In order to help me overcome this deep seated fear, he suggested that it might help if I could share a controlled experience with him. Sitting me down in a comfortable position, he asked me to close my eyes and relax. Peeking out of the corner of my eye I watched him do likewise. Suddenly, I was with him in a stone tunnel, it seemed to go on for a great distance and as it did so, it slowly curved around so that you could not see where the tunnel went. What I could see though was the brightest light I have ever seen. It filled the tunnel with light but its source was just around the bend in the tunnel so that it could not be seen directly. The light began to fill me with laughter. I felt happy, happier than I had ever felt and happier than anyone has any right to feel. I began to laugh out loud and as I did so, tears of joy sprang from my closed eyes. My laughter seemed to become magnified thousands of times and to descend in pitch until I realised that this was not my laughter but someone or something else's laughter. The laughter permeated my entire being so that everything was laughter and light and I knew that I was in the presence of God.

When I finally came out of the trance that I had found myself in, Anantha was already sitting opposite me with a smile on his face and a questioning look in his eyes.

"You see, He is there for you," he explained. "There is no need to be frightened. All you have to do is trust in Him."

As I discovered on several occasions, an experience like that quickly fades just as the memory of a dream fades. At the time that it happens and shortly after, it feels as if it should surely stay with you forever but it fades just the same as consciousness returns to normality. And, with its fading away so too the newly found and almost grasped confidence went as well and as Anantha left, I was ashamed to feel just as frightened as I had been before.

Anantha did help though. Through slow perseverance he got me to a state that I could best describe as toleration of fear. He was also someone that I could share my thoughts and experiences without fear of reproach or that look of horror as your confidant realizes that you really are a freak. Unfortunately, he left the college at the end of my first year returning to Indonesia never to be heard from again.

Before he left, Anantha showed me that the dream world could be used to help me. I was having repetitive nightmares about a big green blob with evil red eyes that pursued me tirelessly each night, even into my waking state. I am sure that the writers of Ghostbusters must have experienced the same thing because when I watched the movie a few years later – there was my green blob sliming everyone!

"See, I told you." he said. "Your fear is attracting things you really don't need. But, there is something you can do about this."

In describing my nightly tormentor to him, I mentioned an amulet that was attached to a gold chain worn around the blob's neck. He told me that I should prepare before bedtime properly and then try to sleep. When I started to dream, I should summon up the courage to confront the blob and break the amulet off of the chain and keep it. "The amulet represents the entities hold on you – if you can break the chain, you will be free." he explained.

I wasn't sure that I could control a dream in this way but I tried. It worked. I was able to do exactly as he said in the dream that night and the blob was gone for good.

"Good job." said Anantha, listening to my story the next day "But, the next one will be much much harder."

"Next one?" I whispered.

"Yes, the next one." said Anantha.

The 'next one' duly appeared more or less as soon as Anantha had departed for Indonesia. Sitting in my student flat late one evening I became aware of that now familiar uneasy feeling in the pit of my stomach and coldness at the back of my neck. I stood bolt upright and began to sweat. The walls of my flat seemed to simply disappear and I could see the entire city of Birmingham from my vista. In the distance was a terrible figure. Clothed in the purple regalia of a churchman it seemed to be fighting against an unseen wind to get closer to me. I began to use some of the self defense techniques I had been shown but clumsily as I was panicking. The figure was now so close to me that I could see its appalling face – a skull with dark eye sockets grinning and leering at me, arms flailing in my direction as it sought to move closer. How long this lasted, I have no idea but a rap at the door broke the spell and the room came rushing back. I slept little that night.

The knock at the door turned out to be Brendan, my friend and flat mate. He had sensed that something odd was happening and had arrived to investigate. Tearfully, I explained my predicament and Brendan, an Irish Catholic, started to draw crosses on each wall of my room with a pencil. He sat with me through most of the remainder of the night. I was moving out the next day, my first year of college over. Goodness knows what the University made of my room after I had left with its penciled crosses on each wall.

Throughout that summer and for the remainder of my college days in Birmingham, the skeletal priest plagued me on and off. The effect was to make me more fearful and jumpy than at any time in my life. But life was bearable, especially when I was able to take my mind off the priest-like specter.

I was a pretty normal student really having a ball, drinking lots of beer and truly enjoying my geology course. In retrospect though, as a person I was probably difficult to bear for most of my fellow students. What to me was insecurity and lack of confidence translated into an aloof arrogance for those around me. When combined with the fact that geology just came naturally so that I was essentially top of the class or very close to it without ever really working just helped foster an image of arrogance. Now I don't want to create too negative of a picture. Again, I wasn't bad or intentionally behaving this way. It was simply my own insecurities, lack of self worth and fear of being left out that made me so intolerable.

A narration of this kind is designed to build a background picture for the reader in order to understand my later experiences as a student of the Servants of the Light School. It would be remiss of me therefore not to admit that at times I felt close to suicidal during this period. I felt unloved, misunderstood, and unsure of myself. Possibly, this was combined with some sort of liking for feeling miserable because at times, I descended into depression and I rather think I enjoyed it. The University physician liked to provide his students with medical help for these sorts of symptoms and for a long time I visited him weekly for counseling. Being someone who fancied himself as another Freud, he really made matters worse by relating all of my issues to sex or rather the lack of it. Despite that, he also readily dispensed 'uppers' and 'downers' to his students who felt under stress. I took a properly prescribed version of speed in the morning and a tranquilizer at night. It actually worked and for a while anyway, I did sleep and a lot of the phenomena disappeared.

It's possible of course that my experiences and my emotional and hormonal state of mind were related. I was a 'late developer' so I was hormonal until I was 21 and grew three inches while at college. Later, I read a number of books by Freud's rival, Jung, that suggested that the link between the occult and our subconscious world is rather closer than might be initially guessed.

At the end of the second year, a geology student is asked to spend 6-weeks during the summer geologically mapping an area as a key component of their final degree work. Usually, students departed in small groups to interesting parts of the UK to undertake this mapping project. This particular year however, when the potential mapping areas where posted, I noticed that one involved spending 6-weeks alone mapping a smallish Scottish island. How they let me have this particular assignment is still a mystery since the senior staff where aware of some of my issues and they were rightly concerned. However, I reassured them that I was doing fine and they finally agreed to let me go.

In reality, my desire to be alone was partly about my wanting to approach the mapping project seriously. I knew that by being alone I was less likely to spend my time in the local pub and more likely to get out and work. Secondarily however, I really wanted to be alone – it suited my sense of injustice and seemed like a suitable sacrifice or penance.

The island of Eigg is located just south of the Island of Skye off the west coast of Scotland. It is a beautiful and lonely place that I have visited subsequently on several occasions. With 50 inhabitants who mostly live on the southern end of the island, my base of operations would be the remote northern end of the island. I neither saw nor spoke to a soul for almost three weeks! It was complete solitude and my first conversation with anyone occurred when I finally ran out of the food that I had brought with me and had to walk to the store located near the southern end of the island. I was proud of myself staying on Eigg. Living in a tent and later, renting a caravan, I was of course freaked out most nights – which were very very dark and long. But I survived and even built confidence over the time I was there.

I was horrified to discover that the required public camping ground on the north end of the island was actually on the site of an old monastery. It was with some relief that, after my tent blew down one day breaking a pole, I was forced to seek alternative accommodation in a caravan. Eigg is subject to quite strong winds at certain times of the year and the caravan was securely tied down with two ropes anchored into the ground either side of it. Each night, I kept a flashlight handy but still had difficulty sleeping because I was totally alone in the middle of nowhere. This was made worse by the fact that almost every night after I finally got to sleep, I was woken up by the most horrendous noise and movement of the caravan back and forth. I didn't dare get out and look to see what it was that might be causing this activity.

Later in my stay on Eigg, my father visited and we spent perhaps the best week of shared time together in our lives. It was great to have him help me with fieldwork and having him around meant I could finally sleep all night long. I told him about the nightly noise and rocking motion that had caused me some concern and he was intrigued. About 4 am in the morning of his first night on Eigg, we were both woken up by the caravan starting to move back and forth with a life of its own accompanied by an eerie grinding sound. My father looked at me and scratched his head before grabbing the flashlight and venturing outside. I heard him moving about for a while and then came a long chuckle followed by a request for me to come out and look. What I saw was a very large cow scratching its back on one of the ropes that secured the caravan! It just goes to show that not every strange occurrence is supernatural in origin and that perceptions can be greatly colored by fear.

Eigg held its own genuine mysteries. Mapping a small ravine one day, I became aware of a presence as if someone were looking at me and, looking up, I was surprised to see an image of a dark haired lady dressed all in blue who was peering across from the opposite bank. I'm not sure who or what she was but I was not afraid of her and her presence seemed comforting.

After that things really began to happen. I heard angelic singing at unexpected moments drifting on the wind. Initially, I thought perhaps it was a radio playing in the distance but wherever I went on that island, it was there. This culminated in a very peculiar experience. Eating a poorly made cheese sandwich on a west-facing beach on the island, I again heard the angelic singing. Louder and louder it got until I had to get up and look around. It was then that I noticed a sword emerge from the ocean followed by a female hand. The intensity of the singing was almost intolerable and a wind seemed to blow around me as I watched incredulously as the hand and the sword came out of the ocean. Of course, I tried to reach for it but could not. I found myself laughing out loud at the ridiculousness of the situation. 'Am I King Arthur?' I laughed but as it became apparent that I could not reach the sword, the singing started to die down and the sword began to slowly submerge back under the water. The experience left a lasting impression and the image of the sword has stayed with me for years.

I must also confess to using whatever these phenomena were for my own ends at times. For example, one evening I met an attractive girl in the pub who was an art student. I wrote lyrics and poetry, dark and brooding stuff, and during our discussions she became interested in my work for a project she was undertaking. This suited me since my objectives were to attract and catch the girl. I invited her over to my flat at the weekend where we would look over my poetry and discuss the project further.

As I have related, I liked to "doom and gloom" and the afternoon that she visited, I was on a particularly low and deep trip. I had developed an attitude of basically being a complete bastard to make her dislike me which would then make me feel even more down. So when she arrived, I was mean and uncommunicative. She busied herself reading my lyrics and poetry finally asking what it was that made me write about such dark and scary things (all excellent topics for her project apparently). I told her bluntly I was psychic and plagued by phenomena that chilled me to the core. She just giggled and said "Oh come on, that's just your imagination and nonsense." "Really," I said "Well, let's see what you make of this then…" I focused strongly on my desire to make something happen – anything happen, quickly sinking into a sort of unblinking trance like state. She looked horrified and I was encouraged to try even harder. "Something happen." I kept repeating to myself when all at once the windows behind me suddenly sprang open as a blast of wind hammered against them. All the papers in the room started to blow around and then the piece de résistance! A print of Leonard da Vinci's last supper, which was stapled to the wall in front of me, but behind of her, suddenly lifted off the wall and drifting against the direction of the wind finally settling on the coffee table between us. The last I saw she was running screaming out of my door!

I did of course have a healthy fear of things that I thought might cause trouble for me. One of these was the ouija board. During a weekend at home I visited a girlfriend's house with a friend. They were playing with an Ouija board and wanted us to join in the 'fun'. I would not and sat in the room next door watching TV while my friend joined in. About 30 minutes later, there was a commotion in the kitchen and my friend came running through the room behaving oddly. The girls were quite upset and concerned. They had been questioning an entity that they thought haunted their house but my friend dismissed the entire conversation as hocus pocus and demanded proof. At that point, his face changed and he suddenly got up and started running around the house streaming tears and saying he was looking for someone whose name we could not make out.

Fearing that something seriously bad was happening, I chased my friend around the house finally catching up with him on the stairs. I grabbed him and screamed 'Come into me – leave him alone.' I woke up later at the bottom of the staircase with wet cheeks. Apparently, my request had been met and for the last 30 minutes I too had been running all over the house crying and desperately looking for someone! It only confirmed my fear of Ouija boards and meddling.

After successfully completing my undergraduate degree, I went on to do research towards a Ph.D. Throughout this time, strange things continued to occur and I remained scared and jumpy, especially at night. Arriving in Glasgow to continue my studies, I was again to meet with another person who claimed to know me.

My best friend had also gone to college in Glasgow as a mature student and he and I shared a flat. To supplement his income, Mike, my friend, had taken a job at a bar on campus. One evening

I had occasion to go into the bar looking for him but not seeing him there, I asked a barman if he had seen Michael. The response I got was very strange. The barman looked at me with a puzzled look on his face and said "Which Michael?"

"Mike, you know, about so tall with dark curly hair." I replied somewhat puzzled.

"Oh, that Michael." came the relieved and somewhat embarrassed response. "Look, order a beer and go and sit down over there, I want to talk to you." said the barman.

Sitting down, I awaited the barman with some interest. After a few minutes he came over, pulled up a chair and sat down. "I'm sorry," he said, "I thought you were asking if I had seen the Archangel Michael." I wasn't quite sure how to reply to that and so after a moment of silence he continued "I need to talk to you; I'll get a break later, any chance we can meet?" I agreed, after all, there was an established pattern here.

Francis, as he later introduced himself, was a Scotsman and a mature student at the college. He had attended a Waldorf school prior to college and was also sensitive but he was comfortable with himself and very confident. When he had initially met me, he had seen, so he said, a very bright light around me – my aura. The sight of my aura had momentarily caused him to make the very strange Michael remark since, with my aura,' I could not surely be asking something mundane. However, he had become aware quite quickly of my condition and he knew that he could help me.

Francis and I met and talked regularly. He exposed me to the writings of Rudolph Steiner and others, and helped me make sense of some of it. More importantly, he tried to help me with the root causes of my persona – my fear. However, whenever Francis and I met, I would always get a burst of energy with the result that I saw and heard all the more acutely and so I was scared. The experiences that I had with Francis mostly took the form of first sensing something and then visually seeing bright lights floating around my room. Sometimes, voices would seem to emanate from the lights that floated there.

Francis and I became firm friends but we lost touch very abruptly a few years after I finished my Ph.D. and I have not seen nor heard from him since. He had told me that would be the way it was shortly after we first met along with a number of other things, all of which have transpired just as he related they would.

Another phenomenon that started around this time was what I can only call automatic talking. When in the right frame of mind, I would suddenly start 'preaching' to my friends. I knew that I was doing it and could hear my voice but the words didn't seem to come from me at all. In fact, I always felt energized when this happened and it would occur in the strangest places such as the disco on a night out where for 20 minutes I would lecture my girlfriend or some other hapless friend, on the true meaning of life and everything. I realize now that I was probably just channeling unknowingly but it sure added to my growing reputation for strangeness.

Sometime about this time, I had an experience which became the last straw for me. Being an impoverished student, my girlfriend and I bought a rather nice jacket in a charity store. Later that evening, when I donned the jacket, all hell broke loose. All I can recall is feeling very cold and then my girlfriend slapped me in the face insisting I take off the jacket. She too had felt the room become cold and sensed a distinct change in atmosphere and apparently, I had changed entirely into some other disturbing persona. It had been an unpleasant experience for her and an unpleasant persona. I felt both drained and sick by the experience and the jacket promptly went in to the trash.

For me, that was really it. It was something for me to be frightened and persecuted by forces that I didn't understand but when it impacted people around me, it just had to stop. For the next 15 or more years, I made a determined effort to block out anything and everything and, as I got wrapped up in the daily grind of work and raising 3 sons, it worked. The phenomena were almost entirely gone.

Even though I no longer seemed to attract unwanted attention, the consequences of living through those childhood and early adult experiences stayed with me. I slept with the light on whenever I was alone.

Chapter Three

The cup that I was given

Although the phenomena were now suppressed and largely gone, my personality was still very much motivated by fear and worry. Having earned my Ph.D., I started work as a geologist working in Aberdeen. By now, I had met my wife to be and spent most of my free time commuting back to Glasgow to be with her. In part, however, it was my insecurity that made me go back to visit every weekend. I know that at times she felt restrained by my actions and my personality, but luckily, she saw the light deep within my soul all the same.

My approach to work was one of subconsciously proving how good I was - simply a response to insecurity and a fear of losing my job. In fact, I was paranoid about losing my job and spent lots of time worrying over my job performance and trying to read all sorts of things in to other people's reactions to me. How much time and effort I wasted worrying! Funnily enough, my fear of job loss finally came true a decade or so later but it turned out to be a blessing in disguise as I used the opportunity to build my own business.

Time passed by and I soon found myself with three sons and living in Houston, Texas. Still worrying, still unconsciously restricting others, and still trying to control my environment with an iron will. I think that this is partly why some people seem to age more quickly than others. It simply takes a lot of effort to behave this way and those efforts must have a natural impact on the body over time. Even today, I still find myself periodically slipping back into my old mentality from time to time when I allow the stresses to build up. My wife calls this the 'old me' and she will gently remind me when it happens.

It's not that I have gone through some sudden revelation that struck me like a bolt of lightning out of the blue and changed me overnight. It has been a gradual and ongoing process, a path that I am still following. I have changed though. Each day, the inner work has an imperceptible impact that cumulatively results in subtle change.

Looking around at the world, I think that most people are totally unaware of what and who they truly are. Occultists have often called this 'sleeping'. The vast majority of us are sleeping through life pursuing some materialistic dream like children distracted by shiny new toys. I can feel myself being sucked in to this quite often now that I am aware of it. Glued to the TV or lusting after a new and faster sports car, our attention gets sharply focused on the outer world around us and that inner voice that speaks quietly to us gets drowned out by the noise of the world. W.E. Butler, a famous occultist and founder of the Servants of the Light, discusses this at great length in his lectures to the Ibis Fraternity[2]. The world is hypnotic and it seems to me that the more we make technical advancements, the more hypnotic it becomes. It's as if we are all on an endless treadmill that gets faster and faster until your attention is simply on making the next step without falling off the treadmill. But quite often, we are subconsciously responding to worry or anxiety and that's what truly motivates many of our thoughts and actions.

Fear of course is a strong emotion and totally irrational. We live in a world that is fear oriented. Just look at the news on TV or in the papers. Fear, like sex, sells and it sells better than sex in my opinion. I have to say that the British TV news is by far the best at fear creation. US TV news is fluff at best and it's performed with a big smile on the presenter's face. But British presenters have a tone of seriousness lacking in their American counterparts that

---

[2] See Recommended Reading section.

chills you to the bone! Just think about it – what really motivates you deep down and what role does fear or anxiety have in your inner make up? In today's world, fear is used to corral us all in to certain behaviour patterns. It's a 'carrot and stick' world but it's a big old stick and a pretty small carrot.

Fear expresses itself as a continuous and nagging worry that doesn't seem to ever go away. For me, I feel the cumulative effect of fear, anxiety and worry as a growing tension that can then manifest as headaches or even worse physical symptoms. It may well be the most powerful emotion, it certainly is for me. Even when I think I am worry-free, there is some nagging insecurity or worry going on in background mode. The problem is that this worry can affect those around you as much as impacts you. It expresses itself as irrational actions and thoughts.

When I was a young child, I used to imagine that I really wasn't here. My body was here but the real me wasn't. I was locked up in a small room and hooked to a machine that provided me with access to the six senses and allowed me to control my body in the world. I was able to see using a set of goggles that were attached to my head. It was a little like playing the ultimate virtual reality game. Sometimes, life doesn't seem very real to me. Later, the movie 'The Matrix' used something of a similar theme that struck a chord with its audience so perhaps I'm not the only one to think this way. However, one must be careful not to go too far the other way and escape in to an inner world at the expense of living in this one. As with all things, it is a matter of balance and perspective.

Another thought that often pre-occupies me is the idea that, fundamentally I am just a cloud of electrons and other particles operating in an environment that is made up of even more electrons and particles. As I walk across a room, what is really happening at the sub-atomic level and what is holding me together? When you think deeply about this, it raises a number of additional questions related to perception. What I see, or rather sense, is actually just an image or sensation created by my brain. Indeed, as light enters my eyes it is transmitted to my brain where it is re-assembled as an image. In other words, my brain is always interpreting what I see, the atoms and electrons around me, in a way that I can understand it. Put in another context, it's the old question of "I see green but what color do you see?" We both call the colour "green" because we have been taught and conditioned that it is green but your "green" may in fact be my purple!

Now the key to this is that my brain is interpreting all this incoming data as images based on how it has been taught (educated) and conditioned to interpret and present them. It's just like a computer that has been programmed to pick out patterns in a constant stream of binary data and told how to recognise and process those patterns. The same concept readily applies to all of the senses. We sense and we interpret based on our expectations and our past learning. In fact, we are never truly aware of the actuality of a thing but just our interpreted reality of it. Just as in 'The Matrix', the character finally sees his total environment is actually just a constant stream of '1's' and '0's' which he is interpreting into his reality, so too are we visualising our environment and creating it with and in our mind.

This concept might be a bit difficult to grasp at first but just think about it and you will realise that it is true. What we see, hear, smell, taste, feel is actually a creation of our brain based on electrical impulses sent through our nervous system. We don't actually see anything, we sense with our eyes and our brain interprets that into an image. In fact, the image is assembled upside down but our brain corrects this for us. We don't actually feel, we sense through touch and our brain interprets for us. Furthermore, we don't even have the capability to sense our total environment and if we can't sense it, we can't interpret it. For example, we can only hear certain frequencies and can't 'hear' some frequencies at all. By virtue of creating other sensing devices such as the radio, TV, radio telescopes, infrared sensors and so on, we now know that our 'world' is only a fragment of the actuality of the environment around us. And, if we can't sense something or we don't know of its existence in order to build a device to help us sense it, we naturally deny its existence.

It is this mechanism of interpretation by the programmed (educated) brain that perhaps partially accounts for cultural differences and differences in outlook between certain groups of people. As a part of a particular group or culture, our outlook and interpretation is coloured by our assimilation of that culture's belief and interpretation system. To me, it explains why two people can take in exactly the same facts and yet reach two sets of different conclusions. Our brain does the work and our mind conceptualises into pictures, images and ideas that we are able to understand. Just consider the amputee who is still able to feel the itch in a missing limb to understand the power of the mind.

However, I also believe that the brain does not interpret strictly based just on our life training and experiences but that it also has access, through the subconscious mind, to a grand and universal reservoir of archetypal images, and other knowledge, that it can also use. This reservoir or treasure house of knowledge and images has been alternately called the Astral Plane and the Collective Unconscious, among other names. It can be accessed using the right methods but these are hardly ever used by the average person. Our ability to do this has been largely forgotten and it only seems to come back at times of mental or emotional stress, if at all. When, under the right circumstances, the mind temporarily finds that pathway to this facility, strange things can and do occur, such as knowing that something is about to happen or that a certain person is on the phone before you pick it up. However, this is usually sidelined to the category of the "deja vu" experience – strange but abnormal. Since we under use, or have lost the ability to use, this amazing facility to tap into the universe, we must retrain the mind in order to regain it.

In fact, to go through life simply accepting our conditioning, our brain's hard wiring if you will, is to "sleep" to the potential that our reality can be so much greater and so much more rewarding.

By being constantly sucked into the day-to-day treadmill of life with all its hypnotic attractions, we never have the time to question. I think that because I already saw and sensed the possibility of other realities, I have always had questions and studying the occult has provided me with a means to break down some of my pre-programming, rewire those circuits in my brain, challenge my assumptions and begin to see the broader perspective of my reality. It is why the retraining process has to be slow, gradual and cumulative. This may also be one of the reasons why occult methods are rejected by many people – they simply do not want to access this strange and often frightening capability.

For many mystics and occultists the world is actually viewed as a purely 'mental' construction. It is a creation of the brain and exists only in the mind of the beholder. Indeed, this concept can be taken a step further to suggest that thoughts can and do create our reality. On a mundane level, of course, thought does indeed create. It takes someone with an initial vision or dream for it to be turned into reality. Watching birds soar through the air caused people to dream about flight and eventually this resulted in the invention of the airplane. Man has often dreamt about going to the Moon and this vision became a reality through the thought and ingenuity of many people. All of these are truly examples of magick at work.

Actually, most people know at least subconsciously, that it is thought that creates their reality. Many people can tell stories about the friend or a relative who goes through life with incredibly bad or good luck and they will often pinpoint the cause for this luck on that person's outlook on life. The person who always sees the world's negative qualities is always looking for problems and they see the glass as half empty instead of half full. In the process they create their own luck, their own reality, and that luck follows them through life.

Since our perception is actually largely visual in that we think in pictures and images, when we day dream we are also being creative through the thoughts that create those images in our mind.

The images have their own reality. A dream also seems real to the dreamer and has its own reality. In fact, occultists believe that these thoughts or visualisations can and do create reality and so does the positive thinking community. Millions of self improvement books have been sold the world over based on the simple idea that positive thinking can impact your life for positive benefit. Even some members of the scientific community now grasp the surprising power of the mind as a force to be reckoned with. This is surely all magick.

In fact, at times, it is actually ritual magick since these positive thinkers will repeat their affirmations and positive statements as mantras that are repeated over and over again in order to change their environment. And that's it. From where I sit, that's all there is to magick fundamentally. You constantly create your own reality and you do it through thought. It becomes akin to ritual magick when you use tools as reinforcements and aids to the thought processes that are being used to create the reality. Its one thing to imagine I am successful but its better to think and act as if I am successful. In order to act as if I am successful perhaps I buy a Rolex watch to reinforce that idea. That Rolex has become a ritual implement in my magickal rite of success.

All of this plainly involves the ability to both use imagination and to visualise. Our imaginings, if visualized correctly and acted out, can become our reality. So it follows that the better that I can visualize, the more chance there is that my thoughts will take root in reality. This is why occultists and magicians have always practiced visualisation and imagination so intensely. Many books have been written on this topic but perhaps the best is that by Dolores Ashcroft-Nowicki and J.H. Brennan[3]. It explains in great detail how thought and visualisation has been, and is used today, by the magician.

I also need to re-wire and re-program my brain to regain access to the treasure house of images and archetypes that exist there. This means gradually breaking down long-held viewpoints and

[3] See Recommended Reading Section

stereotype images to make the mind more open and receptive. More fluid. Just as with any habit, it takes conscious effort over a period of time to break down those patterns of thought and thought processes. It's not easy, especially since it is comforting to accept blindly what we have always believed to be the truth and to continue to look for that truth in the outer world of perception.

Chapter Four

RENEWED INTERESTS

My life settled down into middle aged inertia. I once again started to be attracted into reading books and articles on the occult and paranormal phenomena. I realised that perhaps the best way to confront my fears and worries was simply to face them, analyse and explore them. I had addressed my fear of flying that way and, in the process, successfully learned to pilot an aircraft and even fly solo.

I initially began a search of the internet for information on study courses on self-development and occult matters. I discovered a Rosicrucian[4] organisation and signed up to study its philosophy. It was through this organisation that I was later introduced to the Servants of the Light School of Occult Science in the UK and after studying their website with interest, I applied to take the five year course.

The five-year course consists of monthly lessons by mail. Each lesson also includes intense practical work in the form of meditation exercises. There is also an extensive reading list of books and texts on subjects ranging from mythology to Kabbala[5]. To help the student along the path, the school assigns a supervisor who is available for correspondence and who reviews the student's progress through inspection of the student's diary maintained during the course. Additionally, the school organises various lectures and meetings that can be attended by students periodically, including some ritual magic courses. I have no idea how many students complete the course but I can say that it demands effort, work

---

[4] Confraternity of the Rose Cross (CR&C)
[5] See Appendix A

and persistence. And so it was that I began my work with the SOL. I could hardly wait for my first lesson packet to arrive.

The first few lessons were largely about establishing the basis for the course both in terms of content and of approach. Progress is slow through these initial lessons and there is a natural tendency to become impatient. Despite that, they are necessary and by the fourth or fifth lesson, I was beginning to experience some initial results from the meditation sessions.

In her welcome letter to me as a student of the school, Dolores Ashcroft-Nowicki had warned that some students 'ran for the hills' by the fifth or sixth lesson. That statement intrigued me but I soon began to see why as strange and often frightening images floated into my mind during meditation. My supervisor was quick to point out that this was entirely natural and to consider that the images looked very like medieval church imagery such as gargoyles and the like.

Indeed, these images were largely of faces. It was the eyes of the faces that were disturbing having no pupils! Yes, they did look at times like gargoyles but at other times just like people floating through my mind. There were other images too – swords, battles and armies marching across plains, crosses, other strange symbols and images. Looking back at my notes, these images all seemed either pseudo-religious or were associated with war. I was essentially clearing out my mind, calming and cleansing it for the work to come. I was beginning to exercise new pathways in my mind and they needed to be unblocked, oiled, and cleared all of the garbage that had accumulated there over the years.

Each lesson demands a degree of memorisation of the school's systems. Through daily and continuous practice, the memorisation seemed fairly easy if somewhat tedious. The lessons slowly build a 'working space' in the mind of the student using a set of images and visualisations. In essence, the student is building an inner temple that provides a peaceful and controlled area into which to retreat for contemplation and meditation. The school uses its own set of images and visualisations in its lessons that are progressively developed over the course.

Another occult concept is at work in the school's training - that of the Group Mind. Since each student builds similar mental images during the coursework, the resulting images gain increased energy and empowerment because multiple minds are creatively visualizing the same set of images. The Group Mind is a powerful idea that is sometimes seen at work in the outer world in the unconscious actions of the mob or in the shared values and outlook of a particular culture. Any image that is visualised and empowered by group thought develops a potency and power of its own and it is for this reason that the old pantheons of Gods from the Egyptian, Roman and Greek periods still have relevance to the Magician. They have been charged with the thought energy of millions of worshippers over the centuries.

The student needs to persevere with the basic visualisation and memorisation exercises despite naturally wanting to become a master Magician in just a few short weeks! In times past, this initial training period in esoteric and occult schools was a good deal longer and much more difficult to get through. Whenever I got bored with the process, I would tell myself that this is what I had wanted – a comprehensive training in the occult.

It's funny but my exploration of the occult has also been tinged with a little disappointment. Perhaps I had read too many Dennis Wheatley novels and seen too many Hollywood movies myself, but somehow I really thought that magick would be more wand waving than hard work. What I have discovered is that magick is very hard work and its focus is on the self. There are no real shortcuts and there are a lot of fundamental challenges that need to be faced by the practitioner. I thought that magick would involve conjuring something desired in the outer world but discovered that it is about changing things in the inner world so that it can manifest in my outer world reality.

The school's lessons introduce the student to a series of pre-meditation exercises such as Israel Regardie's Middle Pillar[6] that serve to cleanse, energise and prepare the mind and body for a safe session. Accompanied by reading works from the suggested book list the course can be made more interesting over the first year through those reading activities. This initial period is crucial. You are learning some very basic but important techniques and methods to help with visualisation, meditation and concentration; you are re-wiring your mind and re-finding those pathways that connect you with the Universe.

About twelve months into the course I finally had my first real world altering experience or 'high'. I was involved in a meditation on the very centre of the Tree of Life[7] – Tiphareth – the Tree's central point of harmony and balance. As I meditated, I saw the image of a face. It was indescribably beautiful and radiant. Its eyes were wells of love, hope and wellness. The face was undoubtedly that of Jesus and I was stood with Him in a garden as a crowd of men and Roman soldiers arrived. Jesus looked around at this crowd and I watched as one man came over to him and simply placed a hand on his shoulder as the signal for his arrest. The image then changed and I saw three hills outside of a city and on the centre hill were three crosses and three men being crucified. The middle figure of these men was Jesus.

I watched as dark clouds appeared out of nowhere and the skies opened up just as Jesus expired on the cross. There were earthquakes and lightning but there was also a flash of the brightest light that emanated from His dying crucified body. The light rushed outwards and entered everything in the world. It seemed to hit me also with a burst of energy such as I have never experienced before. As that light entered my body, I was suddenly one with everything. One with the One thing. I knew in that instant that everything is really one and that our individuality is simply an illusion. This feeling and the experience of it is actually indescribable. It

[6] See Recommended Reading Section
[7] Appendix A

made me laugh and cry all at the same time and it stayed with me as a powerful emotion for the next several days.

I was so excited by this experience that I immediately wrote to my supervisor. I had so many questions – what did this mean? She responded that I had had a 'peak' experience but provided no real answers. It is only now that I realise that she could not answer my questions directly because to do so would have been to put her perspective on it while what is important is my perspective and my realisations as a result of the experience. It would have been strategically wrong for her to answer my questions because I had to answer them myself. In answering them myself, the realisations and thoughts would come from me and be mine. That is the occult way. You find your own answers. Your supervisor or teacher is simply there to suggest other lines of research and to help you with the method of investigation.

It was some time before I experienced another of these peak experiences but I found it somehow easier to visualise and meditate after that session. I realized that this whole experience had been like a waking dream – I wasn't driving - it was just happening to me. I also knew that I was making progress but what did this mean? Was I seeing the actual events of that day 2000 years ago? What was that light energy that seemed to emanate from Jesus and penetrate everything on the Earth?

Additionally, I had now learned something about visualisation. When I first started the course, I was very concerned about whether I was doing it right and I had some back and forth with my supervisor on the topic. What was meditation and visualisation actually? There is much discussion of this in books on the occult and magick. However, eventually, I seemed to stumble into being able to do it and despite occasionally questioning my version of meditation and visualisation against what I read as other people's experience, I began to understand that what I do works for me and gained in confidence. I now see that during my life I have in fact spent many innumerable hours meditating without ever realising that I was doing it.

As a child growing up in England, I had quite a distance to walk everyday back and forth to school. To kill the boredom of the walk, I would imagine that I was a pop star with my own band and a song in the top ten. Occasionally, a strange thing would happen. As I walked along singing the made up song in my head and imagining that I was performing the song on "Top of the Pops" (a BBC TV programme),somehow and without knowing how, I would enter a state of mind in which I could actually hear the music and pick out the bass, drums, guitar, piano, and backing vocals. The song took on a life of its own and it was real. Of course, as soon as I consciously realized this, I snapped out of that state and instantly lost the ability altogether finding myself singing in my head once more. After this had occurred a few times, I began to try to make it happen with some success.

Now, when I am meditating, I know if I have reached the right level because a similar thing occurs. Whatever I am imagining or concentrating on, or whatever image happens to arise in my mind, takes on a quality of realness and animation, I am there. For example, I see a pipe and water begins to flow out of the pipe. I can follow the running water wherever it goes without any conscious effort. Suddenly, I hear the sound the water makes and I feel its coolness. I have learned to just go with the flow when this happens because any conscious realisation of what is occurring results in the instantaneous loss of the experience. I also learned that when I begin to see a bluish colour, I am in the right state of mind - though I realize that this could be something specific to me.

Similarly with visualisation. At one time, I screwed my face up with misplaced concentration in an attempt to actually see a picture on the back of my closed eyelids. While I can and do see images on the back of my eyelids, I know I am truly visualising in the right state of mind when I see the images somewhere in the middle of my head. This is a difficult concept to explain, but the image that I see is literally somewhere inside my head as opposed to on the back of my eyelids. It's very similar to dreaming because the dream image is inside your head not on the back of your eyelids. Since I recognised this fact, whenever I can recall a dream I make a note of it in my meditation journal. It's amazing reading back over the journal how the waking dreams of meditation and sleeping dreams both correspond and add to one another!

I have also read a lot about "concentration" in books on visualisation. Many authors discuss how difficult it is to concentrate and offer opinions how to achieve it. At first, I interpreted this as others might and found that in trying to concentrate acutely, I was simply tensioning all of my facial muscles and not achieving anything - except perhaps face ache. After I forgot what I had read about concentration and started to make progress in meditation, I finally understood what was really meant by 'concentration'. I now interpret this term to mean 'stillness of mind' as opposed to an 'acute focus'.

During meditation, one uses concentration to slowly enter a different mental state that is something akin to waking sleep. My body is asleep but my mind is focused and concentrated or centered on the subject of meditation. I am in a mind awake but body asleep state. This mental state is also apparently required to 'remote view'[8] and I have often wondered if remote viewing and astral projection isn't really one and the same thing?

I now understand that imagination is the key that unlocks the ability because once one achieves this state, the experiences that may result from it are triggered by the commencement of imagination. The imaginative faculty is the engine room of magick and the better a person can use imagination the more likely he/she will have early success in meditation. It is in this state of mind that I have travelled both in the present and into the past. I have 'flown' over my parents' home in England from Texas and comforted my wife at home. In the latter case, I was able to prove to myself that the experience was real at some level because I observed my wife crying and sat with her to comfort her. After the meditation session, I went home and found that my wife had

[8] See Recommended Reading section.

indeed been sat on the sofa where I had seen her and she had been crying. She had even felt comforted by a 'presence'.

In this state of mind, I have traversed through my own inner landscapes meeting characters and creatures along the way that held some truth for me. Often archetypal images, I have talked with my shadow (I call him the angry old man or just Mr. Angry) and have embraced my anima; learning much about myself in the process.

A common and ubiquitous image that comes into my mind is that of a sword. I had seen a sword in my beach experience on Eigg as a geology student and this has been repeated over and over again in my meditation sessions. Either the image of a sword would just float up in my mind's eye or I would actually see an arm with a sword arise from a surface of water. I asked my supervisor what the sword symbolised and also posted notes on various occult discussion boards on the web asking for interpretations. What I didn't realise at that time was that I had to discover the meaning of the sword for myself as opposed to from others. For me the sword is an instrument of discrimination and as such it can be used to cut to the truth of the matter. Later, I would use a sword in my mind to do just that.

So just how do you meditate? There are many meditation methods that you can read about in books. What I do is to first make sure that I will be undisturbed and then sit with my back upright and my hands on my lap in a supportive chair. Usually, I burn incense and may play gentle music in the background to create a more conducive atmosphere. Then, I close my eyes and begin to try to relax. One way to relax is simply to focus on each part of the body, starting with the feet, consciously relaxing the muscles there before moving on to the next part of the body.

Another method that I use extensively is to focus on my breathing. I imagine that I am breathing in air that is coloured a nice shade of pale blue. I hold the breath and, as I do so, imagine all the stress and tension coming out of my body into this pale blue air and turning it a bright red in the process. When the air in my lungs is completely bright red in colour I slowly exhale the air and all of the tension that has come out of my body and in to that air goes with it. I then commence the cycle again repeating several times until I feel totally relaxed. The next step is up to you. You can either focus on a question, a statement or a thought in your mind or you can just allow images to rise up.

In the first scenario, I generally repeat the question I wish to ask several times and then stop to listen to what the answer might be. In the second scenario, the issue is to keep from reacting to any images that arise in a way that brings you back to a normal state of consciousness. Just let the images arise. Do not judge them. Do not be surprised by them. Whichever way you choose to go, it takes practice to get results and when you do get results, write them down immediately. Eventually, the process of meditating takes you deeper within yourself until you are in a mind awake, body asleep state.

My initial problem was that I was simply trying too hard and just could not get relaxed. Every time I felt relaxed, my efforts to concentrate would make me tense again. I found myself tensing up my jaw or my legs and spent the entire session just trying to relax! Another mistake that I made early on was to forget about the telephone. When the phone rings and you are deeply relaxed let me tell you that you jump violently and unpleasantly.

As regards visualisation, once I stopped trying to see pictures, I saw pictures. The harder I tried to create an image of anything in my mind the less successful I was at it. Now, I simply want to see something and I see it imaginatively. I don't actually have to 'see' it to be visualising. I can imagine being beside the ocean and recall the smell of sea-spray in the air and I am visualising.

It seems to me that a lot of people struggle with visualisation thinking that you must actually see the image in your mind in as much detail as if you were looking at the object concerned. For me this is not the case. I just imagine the thing and it is there. There may be no actual image since the visualisation may take the form of a smell or an atmosphere and once the imaginative faculty is working, it just takes over.

If visualisation proves too difficult, you can actually 'talk' your way through to visualisation. You simply say to yourself in your mind what you wish to visualise describing it in detail and sort of walk your way through it. This is similar to a technique called 'path working'[9] and I have found that it can be a highly effective method. Path working is a guided meditation using a pre-prepared script. At the end of the day, it is sufficient to do what you can do without forcing yourself to lose the state of relaxation. This is definitely a skill that comes with time, hard work and practice. The key to success is not to give up.

Another thing that you should bear in mind is that on completion of meditation take the time to come back to this world. Stamp your foot and look around you. Make sure that you are awake both mentally and physically. I know this to be true and worth remembering because I abruptly stood up after a meditation session only to fall over because my legs were still asleep! I can assure you that this is painful and should be avoided at all costs. Finally, do write down your experiences in detail after meditation. Like dreams, the information that you access is quickly lost in normal consciousness and even the smallest fragment of that information can prove critically important later.

An example of this was a series of meditations that I was engaged in shortly after my crucifixion experience. I kept seeing and hearing what appeared to be 'AR' or 'AZ' or something similar. I dutifully wrote it down. Reading back through my dairy one day, I noticed that these two letters kept coming up over and over again and so I began asking what this meant. In answer to my question, I found myself in a tunnel with water running in it. I often see tunnels during meditation and so I was not greatly surprised. I had a sword in my hand and for some reason I decided to hack at the side of the tunnel with it. As I hacked a hole in the tunnel I could see blue sky and sunlight outside. When the hole was large enough, I stepped

[9] See Recommended Reading section.

through and found myself on the side of a very steep mountain in the most amazing mountainous desert country.

As I looked around this landscape, I noticed a small huddled figure sat on the mountainside dressed from head to foot in grey robes.

"Who are you?" I asked.

"Asteroth," was the reply.

Chapter Five

ASTEROTH'S DOMAIN

When I first made contact with Asteroth, I was pretty shaken up by the experience. Just who or what was this entity that was communicating with me? I immediately went out and did some web searches on the name 'Asteroth' and the results only served to deepen my suspicions. Asteroth, it turned out, was the name of a demon, but it was also a name that was associated with the Goddess Astarte. Astarte was also known as Astarat and Astoreth and She was worshipped by the Syrians, Palestinians, Phoenicians, Egyptians and other Semitic Tribes. King Solomon had built a Temple to Her as Astoreth, near Jerusalem. Astarte was worshipped as many things. To the Egyptians, She was a Goddess of War, to the Semites, She was a Goddess of Love and Fertility and for the Greeks, She was Aphrodite, also a Goddess of Love. The first thing I did was to consult my supervisor via email. I was advised to acknowledge the entity and to engage it carefully in conversation if I felt comfortable doing so. Putting aside my fears, that is exactly what I did. Over the next several months, I would meditate and seek out this entity on the hillside and sit with her. I never saw her face but always saw her as a small bundle of cloth and completely covered; which just added to my initial worries.

"Who are you?" I would ask.

"Asteroth." Came the reply in my mind.

"What are you?"

"I am of the Word."

"Who is the Word?"

No answer.

"Why don't you answer?" I would ask.

"I am answering you," she would say. "But you chose not to hear."

"What is your purpose?"

"I am here to guide you," She said.

Cautiously over the next several weeks, I developed a relationship with this entity that existed in my meditating mind. I would call her by name and she would be there beside me. After a while, I became accustomed to her presence and began to lose my fear of her. After all, no harm had come to me as I talked with her. As time went on, I realized that Asteroth was either an independent entity that I was channeling or, more likely, Asteroth was a part of me. During this time, I was following the SOL lessons, performing the exercises and writing my notes in my diary to send to my supervisor each month, but I was also taking the time to visit with Asteroth and ask questions.

During one session, Asteroth told me that she wanted to take me to another place, a special place. We were instantly transported to an Orchard. The Orchard was full of small fruit trees and by its edge was some grass that backed onto an ocean. The atmosphere was like a Mediterranean Orchard with small flowers and plants all around and the buzzing of bees under a bright sun. "What is this place?" I asked. "It is your Garden of Remembrance," she replied. I came to know it as 'Asteroth's Domain'.

The grass in the Orchard was yellowish and long – up to my knees - and the trees were quite small and gnarly; spaced intermittently. I looked around but didn't see much because of the grass and the trees but there was Asteroth dressed in a black hooded robe just leaning on a tree trunk. She reminds me of a Merlin-type figure but I never see her face under the hood. When I saw her, she walked over and instructed me to sit down pointing to a bit of clearing where the grass had been flattened and there was a fire burning. I sat and she sat opposite me. I asked her about the garden and she said it was my garden of remembrance. I was a little puzzled by that but she instructed me to be quiet and still – it seemed there was a stream behind me somewhere since I could hear water trickling over stones and I could hear the buzz of bees and other flying insects like you hear in the summertime and also a slight rustle as the wind blew through the trees. For all the world I was sat in what seemed like late summertime in an Orchard listening to the natural sounds around me with an old magician for company. After a while, I asked where I was and why we were there. Again, I was told to sit still and listen. After that, I got the feeling that this was a special place of learning for me. I sat for quite a while feeling the sun on my head very pleasantly until it seemed time to leave.

Diary extract.

From that point forward, whenever I wished to visit Asteroth, I would go to this garden of remembrance and sit by that fire side-by-side with a small huddled and robed figure. Whenever I asked a question, the response was mostly just 'be still and quiet' and in that stillness and quiet would come answers of sorts. As time wore on through the course, I - the apprentice - sat in silent meditation within a meditation with Asteroth as her instructions to me imperceptibly changed from 'sit still and listen' to 'look into the fire'.

My sessions in the garden with Asteroth were in addition to following the exercises in the school's lessons but, as the course progressed, I found that my time with Asteroth was increasingly productive. I did not ignore the content of the lessons and indeed my supervisor would often sharply remind me to follow instructions if she sensed I was wandering, but I would make time to sit with Asteroth and my supervisor seemed to silently encourage it.

After about eighteen months of almost daily meditations of between fifteen and forty-five minutes in length, I had reached a level of comfort with the practice. I was retreating into my inner self and finding surprising landscapes and characters there. Reading through my diary entries periodically, I noticed certain themes and reoccurrences in them. By now, I had realized the value of recording everything that I could of these sessions no matter how small, insignificant, or fragmentary they might seem. I had also created a new standard entry in my diary called 'Dreams' where I recorded anything I could recall of my dream life. There was a growing pattern emerging in my daydreams or meditations - one that I could not ignore and that caused me to work all the harder at my daily meditation.

My imaginings, visualisations or experiences were growing more detailed, varied and colourful. My personality was being imperceptibly changed and coloured by these inner journeys because I was beginning to experience another level of my reality; another level of myself; my true self.

I found that some long held beliefs and value sets were being fundamentally challenged and tested and, if I was serious about my studies, I needed to address these changes lest the sands shifted under my feet too much too soon leaving me on an unstable platform. I think that this is the reason for secrecy in the occult community and writings. Of course, part of their secrecy was due to the fact that belief in the practice of the occult could result in religious persecution, suffering and death. These experiences are also very difficult to describe in plain English. But, I believe that the real reason for secrecy among occultists is that this new level of experienced reality causes fundamental changes in your whole being that cannot easily be explained to a third party unless they too have experienced this path.

Additionally, the experiences take time to assimilate. They come progressively often as intense periods of enlightenment followed by long 'dry' periods. Further, many of these insights and experiences are intensely personal. They are about you. It is therefore wrong to provide too much information too soon to a student of the occult. It has to be discovered and experienced by the apprentice through hard work and not from the pages of a book.

There is no language that can truly describe these experiences. No verbs or adjectives seem fit for the purpose and so we struggle to describe and explain. We fall into a language of symbols, glyphs and half-meanings that others on the path will hopefully recognise and understand. I was told this many times by my own teachers but I was naturally impatient and thirsty for knowledge. Luckily, I did myself no harm early on and I have now built something of a foundation through the SOL course that should serve my future explorations well.

I have also been surprised by the mechanism through which this communication takes place. Asking a question in my mind often results in a response that comes back, not in the form of words, but as a packet of information that unfolds in my head. It is sort of a quantum information packet as opposed to a voice talking back to me. It is as if I suddenly just know the answer to the question and so much more. When this form of communication takes place, I have to break off from meditation and start writing in my diary or I forget the ideas and concepts that came to mind. The answer arrives as a kernel that when unwrapped, explodes into a stream of ideas, words, and symbols. It is a packet of information.

However, let's face it. Here I was having conversations with an entity in my own mind! How could I possibly explain that to anyone and retain any semblance of sanity in their eyes? And yet, Asteroth was as real to me as any physical person and pretty demanding too. She began to instruct me to write. "What do you want me to write?" I asked. "Write" would be the reply (not everything in this work is straightforward and easy to understand I have found out). Over time, it dawned on me that perhaps I should write about my experiences with the school and this was confirmed by chance in conversations with likeminded people. One day, I was asking a friend what it was that I could possibly write about when she said "You have a diary? Surely your book is already written."

Of course, one thing that was really changing over time was my fearfulness, anxiety and penchant to worry. Somehow by following this path under the guidance of the SOL, I was no longer afraid. Partly, this was because there had been no reoccurrence of the strange poltergeist-type activities or anything else during the entire time I had been studying, but in truth, I had learned to face my true fear. I had realized that what I was truly afraid of was me!

I tried to consider all of my different personas today. Saw a light in a lamp with different coloured tints passing between it and me as if I am the light and my personalities are like the different tints. These personalities are as much dictated by my perception of the physical world as anything else. I then realized that often I am almost watching myself play a role. The role may be what I believe that role should be like or perhaps how I believe others perceive it. These roles are many – Father, Husband, Consultant, Friend, Son and so on. I also then knew why I had never seen Asteroth's face because if I did, I would 'judge' her to be something the way that I judge others to be something based on the way I have categorised or classified. She just is. I feel that the light in the lamp – the real me – is just a stream of consciousness that is. I began to realize just how complex a creature I have made myself be in order to cope/communicate/be accepted and perhaps as much as anything else, to protect myself.

Diary extract.

Chapter Six

Asteroth's Apprentice

Today, Asteroth told me to write about love. I asked for more detail and she said 'love as acceptance'. I didn't need any more words because the words themselves conveyed the entirety of this suggestion. This is a difficult concept to explain but it seemed as if the words themselves conveyed the feeling and understanding of love as acceptance. It's as if the words are only a key to a packet of understanding which opens up and engulfs me.

What those words conveyed to me was along the lines that when we are told to 'love one another', we are told to accept one another for what we are and what we have the potential to be. It's a surrendering of one's own ego and viewpoint. A letting go of our own conditioning and biases allows us to see our fellow humans simply as they truly are. In itself, this is an act of magick since it involves first changing ourselves in order to see more clearly - to see the divine spark in each and every person.

If I know myself then I recognise my ego for what it truly is. I place it to one side and tell it that I, the real me, I am in charge here! If I can learn to accept myself through self-knowing and coming to terms with whom and what I really am then I learn to love myself. In learning to love myself I am able to love others through acceptance of what they are and where they are at in their own journey. Acceptance is a process of letting go and as we let go we no longer feel the need to

*struggle. We forgive ourselves and we forgive others
and we learn how to truly love. It is only when we truly
know and love ourselves that we really gain the right
and ability to guide others knowing how to help and
correct without damaging that person's self-worth and
progress. Otherwise, any act may be based on something
less than love; it may be based on our distorted
perspective of our self. Indeed, love is acceptance.*

Diary Extract

I did not look for Asteroth on a daily basis, instead I continued to rely on the SOL lessons and exercises, but even so I began to realize that I had become Asteroth's Apprentice. So just who and what was Asteroth?

It was a meditation on a particular Tarot card that led me to the answer. During one session I had made copious notes in my diary and it was my supervisor who, after reading it, suggested that I had a lot of tarot card imagery in my experience and that it might be fruitful to study the images on the Tarot cards further. It should be noted that the SOL course uses the Kabbala, an ancient Jewish symbol or glyph known as the 'tree of life' throughout the course and that, without going into inordinate detail, the 'paths' on the tree of life also correspond to the Major Arcana in the Tarot pack. As a result, meditation on many of those Tarot cards is actually a part of the course.

One particular card that I meditated on was 'The Lovers[10]'. The Lovers card shows a male and a female with an Angel above them. The male looks to the female who, in turn, looks up at the Angel. For me, the man represents the normal waking self – the conscious person, and the female represents the inner or subconscious self. The Angel is the higher self. So what is revealed by this card is that the inner self is actually a pathway to the higher self. The card shows in occult (hidden) terms that the conscious

---

[10] As depicted in the Rider Tarot Deck – see Recommended Reading section.

self must look to the subconscious self to experience a connection with the Divine higher self – the one thing that is all. Fundamentally, the card also speaks to the important concept of polarity because it shows two polar opposites as male and female (ying and yang, inner and outer, and so on). It also shows a triangular relationship known as the 'law of the triangle' where the two polar or opposite points, when brought into harmony or equilibrium, result in a third point – the tip of the triangle, in this instance, the Angel. Just as a man and a woman, through an act of loving harmony create a child, the right relationship between the inner and outer selves serves to create a channel to the higher self.

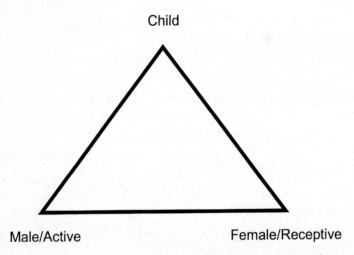

Child

Male/Active   Female/Receptive

Triangle Figure

To understand the meaning of this card further, consider another Tarot card. 'The Devil'. In this card we see a similar arrangement with a male and a female character along the base of the triangular relationship but the Devil takes the place of the Angel of the Lovers card. Looking more closely at the Devil card, it is apparent that, firstly the male and female figures look in opposite direction; inferring that the conscious and subconscious aspects of the person are out of synchronisation. In fact they are chained to a block of stone on which the Devil perches. The male and the female are not tightly chained. The chains are loose and either of the two people depicted could easily escape if they really wanted to. The stone block between the two figures only serves to reinforce the idea that they are separated by some gulf or barrier. Above them ominously sits Satan himself as the King of ignorance. While the Lovers card shows the result of a correct relationship between the conscious and subconscious mind, the Devil card shows what happens when that relationship is blocked. Not only is contact with the higher self, or God, lost but it is replaced by ignorance.

There is something critical being explained to us through the arcane wisdom of these two Tarot cards. For the vast majority of people "sleeping" through life captivated by materialistic shiny things, or indeed, materialistic religious ideals, the connection with the higher self can be lost. The focus of that person is all external-focused on the world of illusions and ignorance. However, a correct relationship between the outer and inner selves brings a connection with the higher self, God, or the Holy Guardian Angel, depending on your preferred terminology. Interestingly enough, there is a strong parallel here with the concept of the 'anima' or 'animus'; being the inner female (on the part of a male) or inner male (on the part of a female).

For me, Asteroth is female and, as such, she may well represent my 'anima' or inner self. She is certainly a connection to my Higher self. She is my teacher and guide and, in many respects, she is my 'Lover'. Throughout my interactions with Asteroth, there is also the idea that she is the culmination of my entire experience and by that I mean also that she seems to have access not just to my experience of this lifetime but perhaps other lifetimes too. To use yet another Tarot card to further explain this, she is like the bag that is carried by the Fool on his journey through the Major Arcana. I am the Fool newly exposed to the wealth of potential experience that may be gained through a life on our material plane and through the choices and paths that I may freely take. Unknown to the Fool, at least perhaps initially, is that the contents of the bag that he carries on the end of his stick contains all the experiences of many previous forays through the cycle depicted by the Major Arcana.

The Tarot cards play a powerful role in my journey because they depict the archetypal journey of the Soul through many trials, tribulations and discoveries. Each of the Major Arcana depicts an event or an experience in the Fool's journey, in our journey, through life. In this regard, they are very worthwhile studying and meditating on. The Magician card is my personal favourite since it depicts its character drawing down energy from the Universe to act upon the four elements of our physical world. It shows the key to any act of magick and demonstrates that we all have the potential to be Magicians. We are all potential Magicians.

Throughout my daily meditation sessions, I have had glimpses of what might be past lives. I say "might" because I sometimes wonder if in fact these past life visions are my own or I am just accessing some particular 'file' in the astral. I don't know. However, the past life experiences, if that is what they are, are interesting and I decided at one point to visit a hypnotherapist that I know for the purposes of past life regression. The session was recorded for later review.

After relaxing into a quiet state of mind I found that I was looking at strange leather sandals on my feet. I felt a sense of loneliness come over me. I was a Roman soldier and I was a long way from home. I could sense my 'uniform' in great detail from the leather sandals to the helmet that I wore on my head. My hypnotherapist moved me through one incident to the next in this life until I dispassionately witnessed my death by drowning as an image in my mind. The last picture that I saw was of a bloated body floating just under the surface of the ocean. In the life that I witnessed I was a no one; a simple soldier with no family, no connections and it was a saddening experience.

Because the session was recorded, I was able to later extract some observations and facts from the tape of session for further analysis and I was very surprised to be able to independently verify most of the details. For instance, I described my lower body armour as a 'dress' of individual leather strips that hung down side-by-side and was surprised to read that this was an accurate description. I also had given a date that didn't seem as if it could be correct for the Roman period. The date I had provided was the year that I had drowned. I was on a Roman galley in a fleet of boats. The boat was on fire and sinking but my thoughts and concerns had been for the oarsmen below decks who could not escape their fate. I discovered that the date tied in precisely with a great Roman seaborne defeat late in the period – something I could not possibly have known beforehand. All the facts seemed to tie in as accurately as could be established and there was simply no way that I could have known this before my regression.

I learned several things from this and subsequent regression sessions. First, the manner in which the images came into my mind and their makeup was identical to the way the images form in my meditating mind. Second, whether or not these recollections are of my own past lives or not, there was meaning and value to them that was relevant to me and my progress as a student of the occult.

In fact, hypnosis is a means to reach the mind awake, body asleep state that we aim for in meditation. Following an occult path is to some extent like undertaking self-hypnosis but using proven and traditional occult methods to guide and focus the self-hypnosis session.

If I am correct, Asteroth is actually a visualisation or personification of the larger me. She is the repository of all the experience I have ever had and of all the knowledge I have gained in many trials and tribulations over many cycles. But more importantly, she also represents the key to the on-going rewiring process of my mind that can connect me with the rest of creation. She is a tenuous link with the Higher Self and in that role she is a teacher and I am Asteroth's apprentice.

The relationship of the consciousness and sub-consciousness pointed to in the Lovers tarot card and that appears to exist in my own relationship with Asteroth also caused me to reconsider the biblical story of Adam and Eve. By seeing this story in a new light, I understand that the story of the creation of Eve perhaps symbolises a point in time when Man awoke to the presence of his inner self. And, if Eve is truly a representation of the inner self, then by eating the forbidden fruit in the Garden of Eden, the Inner self was also awakening to knowledge of the Higher self. Perhaps the story of Adam and Eve is an allegorical representation of the true inner relationship between these two opposites?

My communication with Asteroth is a communication with my subconscious self and Asteroth can be my personal link to the One - God. However, Asteroth doesn't seem to be a necessary connection since I often find that I have access to symbols, archetypes and knowledge through meditation and dreams without Asteroth being a part of the process. Perhaps it is simply easier for the human mind to personify the channel to the beyond in a form like Asteroth or another archetypal figure?

One recurring dream that I experience and have noted down in my diary over and over again is that of an immense and grand house. The house is partly modern but the further back in to the house that I go the older it gets. Parts of it are fortified like a castle and yet other parts are now only ruins. I usually find that I am wandering through room after room in this glorious house that are piled floor to ceiling with the most wondrous objects. The objects include gold, silver and jewels but also ordinary everyday items like ornaments and toys. I am always surprised to discover new rooms including bars complete with alcohol and tremendous libraries full of books. I love this house. I love it with such intensity that I don't want to ever leave it but, somewhere in this beautiful house is a room that I am scared of. In this room something unseen lives that causes my dream to turn into a nightmare. When I find myself in this room, I am thrown around by unseen angry forces that lash out at me.

I know what this house represents. It is me. Each wing or room in the house represents a lifetime of experience and the objects that fill the rooms are things that I 'collected' during that life. The more modern parts of the house are my more recent lives and the older parts of the house more ancient lives. Perhaps the ruined parts of the property are lives so old that I no longer need the support of the experiences gathered during those lives and all that is left is the foundations as ruined walls. The libraries contain my accumulated knowledge and perhaps the bars are places to meet with old acquaintances. But in that house something sinister lives too. Whatever it is it's a part of me.

The woman appears in my mind as a youngish girl – very slim, almost boyish, perhaps in her early twenties. She isn't so much beautiful as overpoweringly alluring and she has a smell about her that is intoxicating. She takes my hand. She seems innocent enough and I am very attracted by her. I can see her face and she is smiling. I ask her about the shadow side of myself and see a glimpse of a face. It is an ugly old man plumpish and feminine in the sense that the facial difference between the sexes appears lost in age. My sense is of someone who is nervous and twitchy. Full of contempt for everyone, dry, wizened and angry. I call him 'Mr. Angry'. He pops out when I least expect it and embarrasses me. Yet the anger and contempt is only the surface of a lot more unpleasantness. I'm puzzled by the rapid nervous movement. He won't look you in the eye – fear. He is afraid of many things. I feel a sense of my fear in him. In my dreams, I sense his presence and then things happen – like I get thrown around by an invisible force. It's the same in waking life – he comes out WHEN I LEAST EXPECT HIM TO. The girl takes my hand again and I reach out for Mr. Angry and find his hand. The three of us are holding hands and I think – here I am. This is me.

Diary extract.

Chapter Seven

The Fool's Journey

The Fool's journey is a long and arduous one, but it is y my journey. It is our journey. For all my formal education, I, like everyone else on the planet, have been conditioned and trained through my life experiences to be who I am today. My fears and other personality traits may have been formulated when I was still very small and through the rest of my life I have been operating to that original specification. Hard knocks have taken off some of the sharper edges and certainly we all mellow with age and experience. As a result, I believe myself to be an intelligent, rational and quite well balanced individual and I am a fool because of it.

Like the Fool of the Tarot pack, I walk along the edge of doom without even being aware of the fact. By taking a contrarian's viewpoint and looking inside to 'know myself' as opposed to looking for the reflection of acceptance in the conditioned reality of the outer world, I gain access to true knowledge. This is knowledge about me and where I truly fit in the grand scheme of things. It is knowledge about who I really am and who I really should be. I have the potential to be so much more than the persona I have created and certainly to be much more than the personas I present to the world.

During my unfinished journey, I have met many characters along the way both in meditation and in my dream world. Perhaps the most painful was to confront a character I simply call the 'angry old man'. The angry old man is a fearful and loathsome creature. Pure hate, pure anger, and pure fear. He is everything that I dislike about myself and more, but we have to live together in harmony.

Tried to imagine my shadow as I would as a small child and then to talk with it. This seemed to work and I asked "Why are you so angry?" and it said "because of you." I asked what I had done and it told me I had rejected it. I explained that until the last few days, I had no idea he existed and now that I knew he was there I wanted him to understand that he was a part of me and that I loved him no matter what. No response. I said that I had been afraid of him because I could not see him but sometimes felt his presence and at other times he had taken me over without permission and that made me fear him even more. I than asked what motivated him. He said "First, I hate being embarrassed. I want to be the centre of attention. I want to control everyone and have them all do what I want." "Anything else," I said a bit shocked. He continued on with a litany of wants. After a while I told him that this was all fine but if we were going to work together and be one, it had to be me that chose what was appropriate for all of us and that there were times that I could use his help. However, most of what he wanted he had to understand was unacceptable. I asked him not to surprise me and to understand that he scared me. We seemed to come to an understanding.

Diary Extract.

By recognizing the angry old man as an integral part of my own makeup, and properly assimilating him into a whole person rather than a fractured set of personas, I become a better, more complete representation of myself. The angry old man is in some senses another polar opposite in my inner make up and, if I can find a way to harmonise these polar opposites, I find the tip of the triangle, the third point that is so much more than the two polar opposites. Besides, there are times in life when we all justifiably need access to the angry old man!

Then there is the woman or girl that I dream about and often see in my meditations too. She is different from Asteroth. She is so attractive, so alluring and yet so familiar. I have dreamed about her since I was a small child and I can still recall many of those dreams so well that I sometimes try to recreate them, re-dream them. She has communicated to me through those dreams my entire life. When I was a child she was the young girl trapped in a room and held captive by the wicked witch that I tried to rescue. When I was a teenager, she was the woman who seemed to make me betray my own values. As an adult, she is a companion that opens up new possibilities for me.

The teenage dream was often repeated. I would always wake up distressed and puzzled by the dream. The setting for the dream was always the same; a big party full of people in different coloured robes. I understood that each robe colour represented worship of a particular God. White robes represented the 'good' God and black robes represented the 'evil' God but there was a pantheon of colours and Gods between those extremes. I wore the white robe but I kept seeing this dark haired and beautiful girl that wore a black robe. I knew that, as a wearer of the white robe, I should not associate with her and so I tried very hard to ignore her. But she seemed attracted to me and after a while I just gave in and together we ran off from the party to be together in a tryst. At this point, I would have second thoughts believing that she was trying to trap me into a betrayal of my God but she would say that there wasn't anything that she couldn't give me, would be mine, if I would only be with her. It was this apparent act of betrayal (I was never strong enough to resist) that made me wake up feeling bad.

For years I had seen this repeating dream as an ominous warning of something to come. It was only through the SOL course and meditation that I realised that I was completely misinterpreting the dream. As a child and a teenager I was endowed by my parents with a strong perception of right and wrong, good and evil. I truly believed that black represented evil and white represented good since this was an aspect of my preconditioning or hard wiring. The SOL course has challenged those and many other assumptions. Black is simply the polar opposite of white. In itself, there is no evilness about it. The two exist and it is us that choose to provide them with a context or a meaning. And it is here that I realized that this dream meant something very different and very important. I was actually dreaming about the reconciliation of two polar opposites of myself – the male and female parts, the conscious and subconscious components. My anima was offering me union and through that union I would become whole and have access to the all. She was offering me a true and valuable gift of a full and complete life experience. But my conscious mind trained and conditioned into a materialistic, externalised view of the world wanted to reject the offer based on a preconception of good and evil. Yes, the thought of a sexual dream encounter with a woman of the 'dark side' was surely the ticket to eternal damnation. How wrong I was.

The Inner Child is another useful inner character for this type of self exploration. By imagining myself to be a child again, the child that I was, I have been able to recall events from very early in my childhood that were undoubtedly influential in my development into the person that I am today. I discovered a child that was intent and serious, something of a loner with a well developed imagination. For example, I found myself constructing soccer leagues, using a dice to obtain scores in the games and then building complex statistics about my soccer league. I was concerned by my preoccupation and inward focus but I am trying to also reconcile that child and assimilate it as a part of me.

I have met many other 'characters' in my astral wanderings through the meditation sessions. Most of these characters I think are an aspect of me wrapped up in an archetypal image but not all. I have also interacted with characters that I believe to be of a different realm. Each of the characters, whatever their origin, have taught me something about myself and I continue to meet with them and others because they still have much to teach.

This is where I see the overlap between the study of the occult and psychology that was recognized by Jung. There are two ways to look at the work that I am engaged in. Firstly, I am a Magician studying occult philosophy and systems or, secondly, I am engaged in a form of Jungian self-analysis using occult systems. Either way, there is little difference.

This is where I become frustrated by the general perception of the occult as some sort of mumbo jumbo satanic ritual cult. There is no doubt that it can be, but those that engage in these practices are not so much occultists as self-deceivers that would always find some anti-social activity to be involved in. What I am doing is self exploration and it's good for the Soul. The work is opening my mind and it is this that is viewed as dangerous. The current trend in organised religion towards blind acceptance of somebody else's interpretation both encourages and relies upon your closed mind. Such religious groups often dictate what you can and cannot believe, how you should think and how you should act, all based upon either a literal reading of their sacred texts or worse still, dogma. This approach can only result in strife because anyone who does not subscribe to a particular path of thought is by default, lost to the cause and often, must be saved. To me, it is this type of closed mind thinking that is behind religiously-based terrorism and intolerance. Yet what makes the world such a compelling experience is its sheer diversity.

If you are thinking about engaging in self exploration using occult methods, hypnosis, meditation or any other method, you will need to develop an open mind. Things that you have been taught as "gospel" truth since childhood will turn into the myths they always were along this path. You are in pursuit of truth – your truth, not some one else's version of it. You may find that many who still cling to the security of their own dogmas turn their back on you or worse accuse you of all kinds of ludicrous sinful and terrible deeds and thoughts. And you will understand why. It is difficult to let loose the chains around your neck. Some just cannot. They are not ready to do it.

We are complex beings. I think that I am an individual, and yet I see glimpses of a different reality in which I am an aspect of the one thing that is everything. My ego, developed throughout life, plainly believes that I am an individual and yet my inner self, through access to other realms and plains of being, seems to be a part of everything. A self-aware piece of the one thing that is all. Truly, we are fragments of the Divine, children of God.

In one meditation session I envisioned a useful analogy for this. I saw each individual as a personal computer. The PC is switched on and sparks to life with no memory of its last use. Its operating system runs local programs and it is unaware of the network of other PCs that it belongs to and knows nothing of the central server computer. When the PC is switched off, it dies. It will be reborn booting up a bunch of background programs when it is switched on again but it has no memory of a past existence. It is only when the user clicks on the "My Network" button that access to the network and central server occurs and suddenly the PC is no longer alone. It is sending instructions to the server for processing there and receiving input and instruction back from that server. The PC thinks it's an independent entity but it is really a part of a vast computing network. It is a part of the one thing.

Meditation and instruction eventually leads to a similar conclusion. It breaks down our pre-conceptions bit by bit and sometimes in a single massive 'peak' experience and the impact of this imperceptibly changes everything about the student. The ego is recognized for what it is and the other aspects of the whole 'me' begin to get the recognition that they deserve.

The Tower Tarot card is isolated on a rocky mountain top. It is alone and isolated; aware of only itself. The Tower seems to have a whole bunch of water spouts at its base and water is flowing out of it in torrents. There was a moss growing around those holes and the water that emerged from them is clear and cold. I heard a voice say 'the clear waters of consciousness are eroding the base of the Tower'. The Tower represents the ego and its views. It feels that it is alone and it is a defensive structure. But as the waters of consciousness flow through and around the Tower, they are slowly eroding its foundations and at some point, it will fall.

Diary Extract.

Chapter Eight

The inner Landscapes

While the SOL instruction has you build a specific inner landscape which becomes richer and broader as time goes on, the student naturally becomes aware of a myriad of other inner landscapes. For some, these landscapes are the Astral Plane, for others perhaps the Collective Unconscious of Jung. It doesn't really matter what words we use to label it, it is the same place. We find there doorways to entire worlds created by the act of thought and imagination. These doorways can lead anywhere; to the world created by the Egyptians with their pantheon of gods or to any world imagined at any time by the human mind.

In this astral world, thought creates in the substratum of reality and, with enough definition and thought energy, that creation can manifest itself in the material world too. Access to these landscapes can be had through various methods including concentration and visualisation of certain images or symbols under the right conditions. Access can also be gained to a vast storehouse of knowledge just as the PC can access the central server if it knows the correct protocols.

The problem with this access is that what you bring back is coloured by your own current make up and programming. Perhaps the PC can access the database on the server but has no local program running that is capable of properly presenting the accessed data. So what is presented to the PC user is a bunch of meaningless font symbols at best and, at worst, just a message asking you to identify the appropriate local program to present the data. This is why the analogy of the Fool is so important. To be foolish might imply a lack of brain cells, intelligence or just a well developed sense of humour but it also means that there is no pre-programmed framework in place that can colour the Fool's experience. Further, the Fool is innocent and childlike and for a Fool anything is possible because there are no rules to follow and no social barriers.

The Fool seems foolish because he is not limited by rules or conventions – the barriers that we create for ourselves in this world. I say that I can't do something because I believe that I cannot or I have been told that I cannot but the Fool has no expectations and does whatever. Not knowing that "it cannot be done" he does it anyway. The limitations that we apply to ourselves do not apply to the Fool. This is not to say that natural laws can be broken but that self-limitations do not exist. As the Creator creates, He is not limited by pre-conceptions of what is or should be. He just creates what He imagines.

Diary Extract.

This is another reason to write everything down from meditation sessions and dreams. There may be information that cannot be understood at the present time but that will become clearer later. To continue the computer analogy, after accessing the server and bringing back data that cannot be presented due to a missing local program, it is wise to store that data file so that it may be opened when the appropriate program is purchased or otherwise becomes available.

In my own inner landscapes I have seen what I consider to be images from past lives. Mostly the people I seem to have been were just ordinary folk though I have seen one life whose escapades are recorded in the history books. Again, these experiences are useful because they tell something about who you are even if they are fantasy as opposed to true past incarnations. My past lives generally seem to fall into the warrior and cleric variety and in both roles I have caused havoc for others. One particularly chilling vision is of me on a battle field covered in blood and sweat surrounded by bodies maimed, wounded and dead. I am exhilarated by it. I am screaming and laughing madly. I also now know that the priest-like spectre that caused me so much fear during my student days was simply an outward reflection of one of these characters.

Interaction with these various characters has many effects on the psyche. Mind is a creature of habit that wants to hold onto ideas and concepts. It looks externally for points of stability to hold on to. The older one gets the more difficult it is to accept change because the conscious mind has been programmed and conditioned and the ego is well-developed and dominant. That's why there is a constant conflict between the youth and older people in any generation. The young minds are still open to and indeed thrive on change whereas the older members of society tend to resist and even deny its existence.

During the development of my inner landscapes, I have built an inner town full of buildings, characters and activities. I can enter this world and explore it any time I choose to. During one session, I suddenly realised that my town was empty and there were no ordinary people there. Sure, I met Knights and Maidens, dragons and Ogres but not an ordinary soul was to be found. Puzzled by this, I asked Asteroth why. She told me to seek out the cave by the lake and to look there for the town's folk. Sure enough, after entering the cave, I found it crammed with people and children. I asked one of these characters why they were hidden away in a cave when there was a perfectly nice place to live in the town outside. "We are afraid." was the response. I struggled with this for a while failing to make the necessary connection between the villagers and me. Then it struck me. The villagers and I have something in common – fear.

Understanding this, I began a dialogue with the villagers explaining all of the reasons why they should not be afraid to inhabit the village. I did this over several sessions and then left it alone for a while. A little later, I was pleased to see my imaginary village populated by people going about their normal business and children playing around the lake. I had had a conversation with myself about fear and by all accounts, that conversation was successful. But there was a second lesson to be gained from this event and that was that we have to live in the real world as opposed to hide in caves. To live, to experience and to make choices demands that we live our physical lives to the full.

What I have learned through the course of study and meditation is that all is not what it seems, and it is well to gradually let go of long-held views and assumptions. In fact, to continue in the work demands that you do so or like the Tower, suffer the consequences of a closed mind.

See a large steel wheel like on an old fashioned steam engine. It's turning relentlessly and is about to run over a person that is laid down in front of it voluntarily. The person laid there looks unaware that he is about to be crushed by this inevitable wheel of change. This reminds me that the mind looks externally for anchors it can hold on to – people it can follow, ideals that it can accept, material things that seem real and solid. In fact, the only true solid 'thing' is inside of us not outside, the only reality the inner self. The outer world of ideas, concepts, things and people can simply disappear in front of our eyes. The man lying there doesn't and can't see it. It seems to me that one should hold onto things and ideas lightly because you never know when the core of that idea will be shown to be false.

Diary extract

Chapter Nine

The Inner Fire

In the Garden of remembrance, Asteroth began to instruct me. She told me to look into the fire that burned there. The fire was a constant presence in my garden and we would simply sit together as I stared into the fire. "Fire is the first born." said Asteroth during one such session. Despite requests for more information on this statement, none was given. So, I continued to look into the fire and quietly contemplate what on earth she could mean. I spent many sessions visualising the fire as best I could, imagining the smell of wood smoke, hearing the spitting and crackling of the burning wood, and seeing the different colours in the flames. Gradually, I noticed two things. Firstly, the fire never seemed to need any additional fuel and secondly, the fire was getting larger and more intense.

Querying Asteroth on the fire's ability to burn without additional fuel, she told me that the fire burned "experience". Further, it was fueled by my own experiences. I realized that what this meant was that the fire was somehow transforming my experience and in the process it was, in a sense, releasing it to pure energy. With my constant and diligent focus on the fire, it was becoming larger and more active. It was getting better at burning the fuel. I was becoming more efficient at transforming experience into energy.

When the fire had become very vigorous and intense, Asteroth said that I should become the fire. This didn't take any effort at all on my part because as soon as I heard the words I became the fire. I was the flame flickering and licking the air. I had no specific location and no real substance. In the act of becoming the fire, it seemed as if it now burned in my stomach region – my solar plexus. I felt the fire energy rising through me. It did not burn, it just felt like energy, and it made me shudder and shake as it burned inside of my body.

If this fire was the firstborn then what did it represent? If I am really an aspect of the All then I am also a spark from that original fire. The term 'spark' is also often used as an analogy for the Spirit. The fire represents my Spirit and as such it is the first born component in my make up. I was a 'spark' or a spirit before I was anything else. As if to confirm my thinking, I saw in my mind a fire bird emerge from the flames – a phoenix. In some way, the act of focusing on the fire, which was burning my experience, was an act of transformation in which a new me would ultimately arise – as a Phoenix from the ashes.

I asked Asteroth about this and she indicated that I was thinking in the right direction. Asteroth it seems represents my subconscious vehicle for accumulated experiences and as we two, the subconscious and conscious aspects of me, watched the fire burn I sensed that something important was indeed taking place. "Are we becoming one?" I asked her. She replied affirmatively but said that this process would take a very long time and that I needed to be patient. It could not be rushed she said. It seemed to me that what had now began was something akin to a process of initiation as the fire melded together two components of myself; transforming the two into a more complete whole.

On the physical level, I was beginning to feel a quite distinct energy flow running through me. It was like heat rising up my spine. This prompted some further contemplation and a then significant realization. Prior to each meditation session, I always performed the 'Middle Pillar'' exercise. Early in my studies with the School, using this exercise, I had built up visualised balls of light in various locations of my body as part of the required exercise but then I had added an extra action of my own. After building up these balls of light, I would imagine two silver cups filled with crystal clear water above my head that poured their content down through the pillar of lights from my head to my feet. When I did this, I could feel energy pass through my body and sense it growing into a glowing aura of sparkling and bright light around my body.

What I was now doing, at Asteroth's request, was a two-way energy flow vizualisation. To begin my sessions, I would let the 'water' energy come down through my body according to the Middle Pillar exercise. Then, in meditating on the fire, I would let that fire energy rise up through my body. I had somehow managed to develop my own unique approach to circulating energy.

Now, as I have meditated on the Tree of Life, I have discovered all kinds of polarities and just how important polarity is. As related previously, the stresses between any two polar points result in the emergence of yet a third point and thus we have a triangle. It's probably helpful to illustrate this concept with some examples. Consider the colours black and white. They are two polar extremes along a rainbow of colour and, in fact, while white is the presence of all colours, black is the absence of any color so they represent the extreme points of a range of colours dictated by the progressive introduction of colour. Now somewhere between the absence of color and the presence of all colours is a point of harmony or equilibrium. That point is some combination or harmonisation of the two extremes; black and white. This relationship can be expressed as a triangle.

Perhaps a better example is sex. In this case, the two polar opposites are naturally male and female and the act of bringing the two together in equilibrium results in new life – a child. So here is another triangle with the basal polar points being male and female and the third point, the apex of our triangle, is a child. As the psychologist Jung said 'In the third, the tension is resolved and the lost unity is restored'. Because there are two polar points in almost any situation, there are always two potential extremes or polar opposites and a path of equilibrium between them. The harmonisation or reconciliation of the two polar points results in the creation of a third point which restores the relationship or tension between them. Opposites attract each other and when these two opposite forces are reconciled in harmony, something bigger is created.

During these contemplations on polarity, I have also discovered that there can be both a horizontal and a vertical polarity. The symbol of the equal armed cross represents this concept very well with its vertical axis drawn between two vertical polar opposites and its horizontal axis drawn between two horizontal polar opposites. The result of this relationship is that a central point is formed at the point of intersection of the two lines in the cross. That point represents the point of both horizontal and vertical equilibrium.

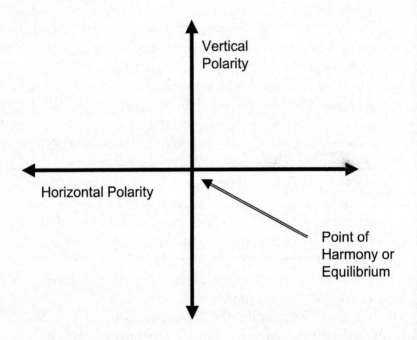

A thought occurred to me during a meditation on 'The Hanged Man' Tarot card. Asteroth instructed me to think about the concept of vertical polarity and for some reason I started to map out the male and female reproductive organs in my mind seeing that these form two particular triangles. For the male, the testes form the base of the triangle and therefore the horizontal

polar opposites while the third point is naturally the penis hence we have an upward facing triangle. For the female, the ovaries form the two points at the base of the triangle and the horizontal polar extremes while the vagina forms the third point and hence a downward facing triangle. Interestingly, the male triangle which points upward is also the symbol for elemental Fire while the female symbol of a triangle pointing downward is the symbol for elemental Water. When these two triangles are combined one over the other we have the hexagram which is a symbol of perfect harmony.

Diary Extract.

Further contemplation of this relationship prompts another thought. That is that there is yet another polarity implicit here that can be thought of as 'in-out' or the third axis of depth in three-dimensions. The third point in each of the two triangles forms this point of 'in-out' polarity (for example and perhaps rather crudely; penis-vagina) and the result of this 'in-out' polarity is to either convert force into form or vice versa (continuing the example, it is this interaction that takes force in the form of intent to procreate and turns it into form; a new child).

This led me to think about Fire and Water at length. Fire is active in that it takes form (fuel) and turns it into force (heat and light) whereas Water is both passive and receptive. Water as the great bitter sea evokes thoughts of the womb and the creation of form from the forces of procreation. Further, Water is the element in which life forms first evolved from basic chemicals and, one assumes, the action of forces such as lightening and heat.

Meditating on Fire and Water and this implicit 'in-out' polarity resulted in an idea for a ritual[11]. If water is passive and receptive, perhaps one can use this polarity as ritual and 'attract' things in to the water. To do this, I visualise a bowl of crystal clear water, energized by moonlight and then see it attracting what I desire into itself. Afterwards, I see myself drinking this energised water.

---

[11] See Appendix B

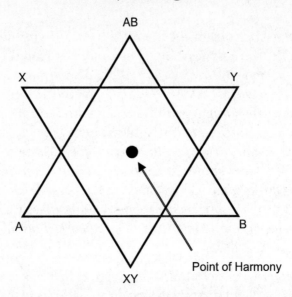

I have had some success with this as visualisation but I generally use it to attract qualities as opposed to material things, for example, increased understanding of my fellow humans. I suppose that what I am doing might be described as polarity magick. One can also use Fire in a similar way except that the visualised fire is used to burn up and dispel unwanted emotions, memories and aspects of yourself.

Polarity has now become a major concept that I continue to meditate on and to try to understand. Everywhere I look, I see examples of polarity and the more that I think about it, the more inclined I am to look for that middle ground and its harmony. In my meditations, I found that I was now practicing a visualisation that reflected this hexagram of balance. I started out using the Middle Pillar and bringing down the water force and then later visualizing an upward movement of the fire force. What might this mean and why had I somehow been led in to this practice?

The 'Middle Pillar' exercise actually operates using two different schemas; first, the balls of light that one visualises can be taken to represent the sephira of the tree of life and secondly, these balls of light and the sephira on the middle pillar can be roughly equated with the chakra system of energy centres. By imagining the water energy descending through the middle pillar of the tree of life superimposed on my body, I am bringing that energy down through my body and its system of energy centres or chakras. In the fire visualization, I am seeing the fire in the solar plexus; a region that corresponds specifically to an energy centre and then letting that fire energy rise up through that same middle pillar of the Tree of life and through the other energy centres in my body. These two forces play an important role in preparing the body and the mind winding up and down the spine in opposite directions. This fire energy can also be equated with 'kundalini[12]', the serpent force of awakening.

Research and reading tells me that deliberate stimulation of kundalini can be very dangerous but the gradual working of this energy is also a key component in self development. Asteroth is showing me a method of gradually building the circulation of energy in my body and spirit. She told me that this would take a long time because the only safe way to clean out and activate the energy centres is slowly. The energy work supplements and supports my inner journeys of self discovery and prepares me for further exploration. The two aspects of this work – energy circulation and meditation - develop progressively together supporting one another. Each has an aspect of unblocking, clearing away and 'rewiring'. Each progressively enhances and develops my ability to connect with the Universe or the Higher self and in the process, know myself, understand my true potential and become a more complete and unified person. I am uniting the polar forces and polar archetypes or personas and in the process, I am enhancing and building the strength of the tip of my own triangle – my Higher self.

The voice was saying to be patient, that my chakras or energy centres are beginning to work again and I got the impression of windmills with sails rotating. Different coloured windmills, some turning slowly and

---

[12] See Recommended Reading section.

others with colour returning but no motion at all. I am an energy system and my connection with the one is through the receipt and flow of this energy. We have lost our ability to connect in to the power source and we feel alone and isolated. As I continue to work the connection is rebuilt, the energy is beginning to flow and that connection is being made.

Diary Extract.

Chapter Ten

PUTTING IT ALL TOGETHER

After a short while, I imagined being with Asteroth and
there we were. I asked about being attuned with the
will of God. She stood with me, arm around my
shoulder and pointed to some trees. "Does the tree not
express the will of God?" she asked. "Look how the
trees grow towards the light, tall, strong and straight.
Do you see them struggling to break away from the
will of God and grow sideways?" I saw a terribly
deformed and frail tree. "OK – but how does that apply
to me?" I asked. "Stop struggling and listen. Attune to
your inner self, become who you truly are and stop
struggling," She said.

Diary Extract.

I had started out on my life journey looking for answers to
questions that I could not form. I have now found that those
answers actually lie within me and have been there the whole
time waiting for me to tap into them.

During my childhood years, I had experienced frightening and
spontaneous phenomena that I now understand to have almost
certainly had their basis and origin within me. For some reason I
was born with my inner eyes and ears open - perhaps all children
are? It might have been my parents' acceptance of this fact, based
largely on my father's own similar experiences that meant that,
not only were these capabilities never shut down, but they were
almost encouraged though without any true understanding of their
nature. Most parents would have 'trained' their child to shut down
these faculties naturally during the up bringing process. It is true

that many children have imaginary friends but they 'grow up' and eventually the imaginary friend becomes just a fond memory of childhood. On the other hand, my parents may actually have attempted to suppress this side of me but there was something more permanent about my version of these faculties. Either way, they were not successfully suppressed during my early childhood.

There can also be no doubt that I encouraged the persistence of these phenomena through my fascination with them that was reflected in the book reading and the other research that I did. I was stimulating the faculties through that interest. However, I believe that I was neither ready for the activity nor was I in a situation where there was any other person that could help and guide me through them. Consequently, as I grew older, the experiences and my reaction to them resulted in a developing fear and insecurity. As my hormones kicked in all hell broke loose but it was I that was the cause. I was a walking energy generator completely out of equilibrium and with no way to naturally earth or discharge those forces. Like a build up of static electricity that discharges periodically with visible results, I inadvertently made things happen. Perhaps this is also the basis for poltergeist type activity?

I believe that my fear and openness really were attracting the unwanted flotsam and jetsam of the astral world. Quite often, I was projecting characters from my own uncontrolled inner landscapes and they appeared as visible phantasms to me. Other times, I was attracting entities that have their own form of existence on the astral plane. I was probably lit up like a lighthouse on their side of reality. I also believe, that under these circumstances, others in close proximity to me could subconsciously pick up on these projections and, in the process, see and experience them too.

Perhaps as that lighthouse shining with uncontrolled intensity, I attracted others such as Anantha and Francis to me. They saw my predicament and felt that they could help. It is entirely natural and right for light seekers on the path to help one another.

*When you enter the pool, the surface is absolutely calm
but your body movement causes ripples and activities
on the surface. The more you thrash around the more
the waves and ripples grow in intensity and knock you
off track. The more you fight the more ripples and waves
and the harder it gets. Go with the flow, align yourself
with the will of the Creator and minimise the waves.*
Diary Extract.

I have come to believe that the chaotic phenomena that I
experienced were as a result of being out of balance. The natural
flow of my psychic energy was 'blocked' or disrupted. My mind
was cluttered with junk and the circuits periodically became
unstable. The sensations that occurred to me as a result of this
were in the form of disturbing feelings, emotions, visions, voices
and poltergeist-type activity.

However, like most people, I was also 'sleeping' and as life
went by at a rapid rate of knots, I was dragged deeper and deeper
in to the hallucinatory world of living a daily life. My inherent
interest in the 'occult' and curiosity regarding my past experiences
– even the fact that I could still see shining auras of light around
other people from time to time, maintained a passing interest in
the occult and paranormal. But it was my dreams that spoke to
me and began to wake me up. It was if my subconscious self was
trying to remind me of its existence saying 'Don't forget me. We
two can be more than we are."

In fact, just recently I had a reminder of how the subconscious
mind can remind the conscious mind of its existence through
dreams. Being very busy both at work and at home, I suddenly
found that I had not meditated for several weeks; dropping a
daily habit of the last four years without even realising it. Somehow
I had been distracted back into my own waking dream of running
back and forth to the office and ferrying the kids around. I felt
tired and lacking the resilience that I usually had and realized that
it was because I had forgotten to take those 20-40 minutes each
day to meditate.

But what truly woke me up again was my dream life. I found that I was having numerous vivid dreams of that most beautiful girl. Her appearance may change and the context of the dream itself may also change, but I know this girl intimately. We have spent a lifetime together. When I awake, I lay a few moments trying to recollect and savour the dreams knowing that she represents my female inner self. Whenever I dream of her, it is because I am ignoring her in my life. She is saying "wake up and acknowledge me." She is my inner soul life and she is the conduit to my higher self. Thank goodness we have a relationship in which she can remind me!

What I have also discovered is that the true path to knowledge is to be found within ourselves. While most people naturally look outwards for guidance and knowledge, I have discovered a world rich with archetypal characters and places that is an integral component of me. I have begun to discover the true relationship between my conscious and subconscious selves, and I am working to restore the balance between these characters so as to build a better and more stable whole. I have come to believe that I am undergoing a form of self analysis akin to psychotherapy, a personal transformation similar to alchemy. I am not just working on my inner soul life, but I am also reflecting the increasing inner harmonisation with necessary energy work. The energy work shown to me by my own inner guide: Asteroth. The energy work is helping to create a complete environment of balance.

I have also understood that I must work to reflect and manifest these changes externally, express them in the outer physical world. The physical world is just as holy and sacred as the inner world - it is a part of the One thing too. It is there that we make decisions and choices and have to face up to the consequences of our own actions. It is there that we have and can use free will. The inner work changes our view of the external world because we are recreating it and reinventing ourselves progressively. I have become the Magician of the Tarot working on the four elements of the world with energies brought down from above. As the Fool, I am working my way through the cycle of life to discover that I truly am the Fool.

What has happened is the beginning of an internal and external alchemy and my soul is being enriched by it. Many of my old perceptions have been fundamentally changed and I will never be the same. I am more positive and I am more willing and capable of following my goals and objectives. When I feel fear, I rise to confront it knowing that this is the way to break its power over me. I am becoming a more complete and unified person possessing a better understanding of my own true nature and vast potential.

Yes, I am waking up.

I see a Blacksmith – he momentarily looks up at me as if he knows I am there and then continues beating the metal that he is working. He takes the metal, heats it until it is white hot and then works it into shape before thrusting it into cooling water only to begin the process again. He is using fire and water. It his will that is shaping a sword from the heated metal using the two elements of fire and water. I am a Blacksmith and I am working on my own instrument with fire, water and will.

Diary extract.

The Hanged Man

Above me a point
Below me its reflection in matter
The sun and the moon to either side
I am the centre of a circle
Hanging in space

Here there is no motion
All is timeless and harmony
The centre of a circle but wait
I am slowly rotating
Hanging in space

I have become one
With the all that is and is not
At the centre of the circle of life
Soon I will be upside down
Hanging in space

As the Hanged Man
I gain new perspective
The above is now my below
And the below my above
Hanging in space

Recommended Reading

Ashcroft-Nowicki, Dolores and Brennan, J.H. *Magical Use of Thought Forms: A Proven System of Mental and Spiritual Empowerment* (Llewellyn Publications, 2001).

Ashcroft-Nowicki, Dolores. *Illuminations: Mystical Meditations on the Hebrew Alphabet: The Healing of the Soul.* (Llewellyn Publications, 2003).

Ashcroft-Nowicki, Dolores. *The Shining Paths.* (Thoth Publications 1997, www.thoth.co.uk)

Ashcroft-Nowicki, Dolores. *First Steps in Ritual.* (Thoth publications, 2005).

Ashcroft-Nowicki, Dolores. *Highways of the Mind: The Art and History of Pathworking.* (Aquarian Press, 1987).

Ashcroft-Nowicki, Dolores. *Sacred Cord Meditations.* (Thoth Publications, 2005).

Brennan, J.H. *Astral Doorways.* (Thoth Publications, 1996).

Brennan, J.H. *Discover Astral Projection: How to Achieve Out-of-Body Experiences.* (HarperCollins, 1991).

Butler, W.E. *Magic: Its Ritual, Power and Purpose.* (Thoth Publications, 2001).

Butler, W.E. *Apprenticed to Magic.* (Thoth Publications, 2002).

Butler, W.E. *Lords of Light: The Path of Initiation in the Western Mysteries: The Teachings of the Ibis Fraternity.* (Destiny Books, 1990).

Butler, W.E. *Practical Magic and the Western Mystery Tradition.* (Thoth Publications, 2002)

Butler, W.E. *How to Develop Clairvoyance.* (Thoth Publications, 2002).

Butler, W.E. *How to Read the Aura.* (Thoth Publications, 2003).

Case, Paul Foster. *The Tarot: A Key to the Wisdom of the Ages.* (Builders of the Adytum, 1990).

Fortune, Dion and Knight, Gareth. *An Introduction to Ritual Magic.* (Thoth Publications, 1997).

Fortune, Dion and Knight, Gareth. *The Circuit of Force.* (Thoth Publications, 1998

Fortune, Dion and Knight, Gareth. *Principles of Hermetic Philosophy* (Thoth Publications, 1999)

Fortune, Dion and Knight, Gareth. *Practical Occultism.* (Thoth Publications, 2002).

Fortune, Dion. *The Mystical Qabbalah* (Williams and Norgate, 1935).

Hall, Manly P. *Melchizedek and the Mystery of Fire.* (Philosophical Research Society, 1966).

Jung, C.G. *Psychology and Alchemy.* (Princeton: Princeton University Press, 1968).

Knight, Gareth. *A Practical Guide to Qabalistic Symbolism.* (Helios Books, 1965).

Knight, Gareth. *The Practice of Ritual Magic.* (Thoth Publications, 2005).

Miller, Richard and Miller, Iona. The *Modern Alchemist: A Guide to Personal Transformation.* (Phanes Press, 1994)

Regardie, Israel. *The Art of True Healing: The Unlimited Power of Prayer and Visualization.* (New World Library, 1932).

Steiner, Rudolf. *How to Know Higher Worlds.* (Steiner Books, 1994.)

Stewart, R.J. *Living Magical Arts.* (Thoth Publications, 2005).

Stewart, R.J. *Advanced Magical Arts.* (Thoth Publications, 2005).

Targ, Russell. *Limitless Mind: A Guide to Remote Viewing and Transformation of the Consciousness.* (New World Library, 2004)

The Three Initiates. *The Kybalion: A Study of the Hermetic Philosophy of Ancient Egypt and Greece.* Replica Books, 2003).

Other Useful Resources

Tarot Decks

The Rider Tarot Deck designed by Paula Coleman Smith under the direction of Arthur Edward Waite. US Games Systems, Inc.

Web Resources

Suppliers of rare, often unobtainable second-hand book and some new - www.magis.co.uk

Asteroth's Domain – www.asterothsdomain.com

Servants of the Light – www.servantsofthelight.org

Confraternity of the Rose Cross – www.crcsite.org

Builders of the Adytum – www.bota.org

Appendix A - The Tree of Life

The Tree of Life is a glyph or diagram that shows the arrangement of ten interconnected spheres (called *sephiroth or sephira (plural)*) representing the organisational system of the Jewish Kabbalistic tradition. The Tree of Life is variously considered to be a map of the universe and of the psyche, and to depict the order of the creation of the cosmos, and a path to spiritual illumination. The ten spheres are connected by paths assigned to the twenty two letter-numbers of the Hebrew alphabet. It is a mystical map of how the world works, how the person works, how life works. Each of the ten spheres has a name that directly identifies the sephira and the ideas that this sephira represents. The various names of the sephiroth are derived from Scripture.

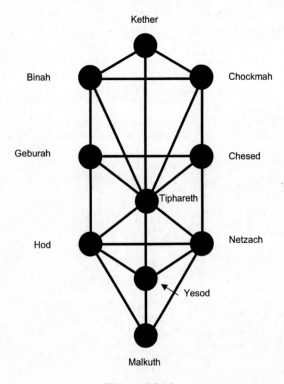

Tree of Life

The Tree of Life depicts the ten emanations of God moving progressively down the tree in the path of creation from the most esoteric point of manifestation to the emanation of God in physical reality. Each *sephiroth* is considered as holy as all of the others irrespective of its position since the whole tree represents God and his creation. As a result, our physically manifest life is just as holy and as worthwhile as our spiritual life.

The Tree of Life can also be used as a reference guide to creation since each *sephiroth* and each path on the tree may be associated to some set of correspondences such as Tarot cards, the planets or virtually any other system. It can be used as a vast filing cabinet of exoteric and esoteric information providing a way for the student to access that information.

For more information on the Tree of Life and the Kabbala, see the suggested reading section.

Appendix B - Fire and Water Meditation

To begin these meditation exercises, find a quiet location where you will not be disturbed and seat yourself comfortably, preferably upright with a straight back. Burn some incense or play gentle music in the background as you desire. Spend about 5-10 minutes getting relaxed and then begin.

Water Meditation

You are seated on an endless flat plain. All around you, the plain disappears into the distance and above you hangs a large and full bright Moon in a darkened sky. It is quiet and dark except for the silvery coloured moonlight which casts no shadow on the flat surface on which you find yourself.

In front of you sits a small but ornate silver cup. As you look at the cup it reflects the silver moonlight back towards you and you can see the reflection of the full moon in its metal. Inside the cup is clear crystal stream water that you collected earlier. As the moonlight shines down and into the cup you know that it is filling the water in the cup with lunar energy. You watch as the water in the cup gradually takes on a bluish silver light of its own as it absorbs the Moon energy.

You watch this energy and the light dancing on top of the water and you know that the water is being energised under the full moon. After a while, you see that the water has now become so energised that it is emitting a pale blue white light of its own.

Knowing that the water is now ready to accept your desires, you begin to see that the energised water is attracting all that you desire as qualities about yourself into it. For quite a while, you watch as these images arise in front of you and then are slowly sucked into the water.

When you feel ready, you will take the cup and giving thanks to the creator, you drink the water. It is cold and it tastes good. As the water enters your body you feel an energy filling you up and you know that the water has healing qualities both for your body and soul. You know that in drinking this water energised by moonlight and filled with the qualities that you desire to build within yourself that even now you are changing. Feel the change take place within you.

Fire Meditation

You are seated on a beach. On one side you are aware of the ocean as small surf waves break on the sandy shore. There is a gentle breeze blowing off the ocean. In front of you a beach fire burns. You watch as the flames rise occasionally blown by the wind. You see the colours of the fire, reds, oranges, purples and greens and you can feel the heat on your face. You can hear the crackle, popping and spitting sounds as the fire burns through the driftwood fuel.

As you sit, the fire grows bigger and bigger as it burns through the driftwood. You can feel the heat on your face getting hotter but occasionally there is no heat at all as the onshore breeze blows the flames temporarily way from you. You feel connected to the fire as it burns. It warms you and protects you from any wild beasts that might be around.

When you can see the fire in as much detail as possible imagine that you are throwing any unwanted aspects of yourself on to the fire. As you do so, the flames jump higher and higher as it burns this new source of fuel. Feel these unwanted aspects of yourself diminish as they are burned on your fire. Smell the smoke that arises as more acrid and know that the flames are turning your burden into energy that you can use.

When you feel ready, give thanks to the Universe for taking your unwanted burden as a gift in the form of heat, light and smoke. Feel lighter and energised by the experience.

Index

Other titles from Thoth Publications:

THE SHINING PATHS
by Dolores Ashcroft-Nowicki

An Experiential Journey through the Tree of Life.

A unique collection of magical pathworkings based on the thirty-two paths of the Qabalistic Tree of Life.

Since it was first published *The Shining Paths* has become a classic of its kind, and an invaluable aid for both students and teachers.

Pathworking is the old name for what are now known as Guided Meditations. They are specifically designed visualisations into which the mind-self is projected into an inner world of learning events and situations which with training can become a complete sensory experience.

Dolores Ashcroft-Nowicki is one of the best known and most respected of contemporary Western occultists. In this book she offers a unique collection of pathworkings based on the Qabalistic Tree of Life. Each working is preceded by a discussion on the correspondences, experiences, and symbology of that path.

Dolores Ashcroft-Nowicki is a third generation psychic sensitive and a symbiotic channeller, she has worked with magic since childhood. A student of the late W.E.Butler, she was one of the Founders of The Servants of the Light School of Occult Science, of which she is now the Director of Studies. She travels the world extensively lecturing and teaching on all aspects of occultism, bringing to her students the accumulated knowledge of over half a century of study and practice.

ISBN 1-870450-30-2

PRINCIPLES OF HERMETIC PHILOSOPHY
By Dion Fortune and Gareth Knight

Principles of Hermetic Philosophy together with *The Esoteric Philosophy of Astrology* are the last known works written by Dion Fortune. They appeared in her Monthly letters to members and associates of the Society of the Inner Light between November 1942 and March 1944.

Her intention in these works is summed up in her own words: "The observations in these pages are an attempt to gather together the fragments of a forgotten wisdom and explain and expand them in the light of personal observation."

She was uniquely equipped to make highly significant personal observations in these matters as one of the leading practical occultists of her time. What is more, in these later works she feels less constrained by traditions of occult secrecy and takes an altogether more practical approach than in her earlier, well known textbooks.

Gareth Knight takes the opportunity to amplify her explanations and practical exercises with a series of full page illustrations, and provides a commentary on her work

ISBN 1-870450-34-5

*   *   *   *   *

THE STORY OF DION FORTUNE
As told to Charles Fielding and Carr Collins.

Dion Fortune and Aleister Crowley stand as the twentieth century's most influential leaders of the Western Esoteric Tradition. They were very different in their backgrounds, scholarship and style.

But, for many, Dion Fortune is the chosen exemplar of the Tradition - with no drugs, no homosexuality and no kinks. This book tells of her formative years and of her development.

At the end, she remains a complex and enigmatic figure, who can only be understood in the light of the system she evolved and worked to great effect.

There can be no definitive "Story of Dion Fortune". This book must remain incompete and full of errors. However, readers may find themselves led into an experience of initiation as envisaged by this fearless and dedicated woman.

ISBN 1-870450-33-7

PRACTICAL MAGIC AND THE WESTERN MYSTERY TRADITION
Unpublished Essays and Articles by W. E. Butler.

W. E. Butler, a devoted friend and colleague of the celebrated occultist Dion Fortune, was among those who helped build the Society of the Inner Light into the foremost Mystery School of its day. He then went on to found his own school, the Servants of the Light, which still continues under the guidance of Dolores Ashcroft-Nowicki, herself an occultist and author of note and the editor and compiler of this volume.

PRACTICAL MAGIC AND THE WESTERN TRADITION is a collection of previously unpublished articles, training papers, and lectures covering many aspects of practical magic in the context of western occultism that show W. E. Butler not only as a leading figure in the magical tradition of the West, but also as one of its greatest teachers.

Subjects covered include:

What makes an Occultist
Ritual Training
Inner Plane Contacts and Rays
The Witch Cult
Keys in Practical Magic
Telesmatic Images
Words of Power
An Explanation of Some Psychic Phenomena

ISBN 1-870450-32-9

TALISMANS & EVOCATIONS OF THE GOLDEN DAWN
by Pat Zalewski

Practical Magic Techniques of the Golden Dawn Revealed! Founded in 1888 by legendary magicians Wynn Westcott and S.L.MacGregor Mathers, the Golden Dawn has been a major influence on the development of Western Magic. Although the material which inspired adepts such as Aleister Crowley and W.B.Yeats has been available, until now there has been little explanation as to how this group preformed its rites of ritual magic.

Now at last Pat Zalewski, himself an adept within the Golden Dawn system, has revealed secrets that have never before been published or which were only communicated orally to a handful of select pupils.

For years people have known that the Golden Dawn adepts could summon spirits so that they could be seen, but no one could explain how they did it. Likewise their techniques of manufacturing and empowering talismans were a closely guarded secret until now.

Here readers will learn the secrets of evocation and how to make Talismans of Power. This book is a very valuable tool into understanding the practical considerations of Golden Dawn ritual magic at its best. It is a must for serious Golden Dawn students.

Mr.Zalewski's books are a gold mine for anyone interested in the Golden Dawn or practical magic.
- V.H. Fr.I.U.S.
Hermetic Order of the Golden Dawn

ISBN 1-870450-36-1

THE WESTERN MYSTERY TRADITION
By Christine Hartley

A reissue of a classic work, by a pupil of Dion Fortune, on the mythical and historical roots of Western occultism.

Christine Hartley's aim was to demonstrate that we in the West, far from being dependent upon Eastern esoteric teachings, possess a rich and potent mystery tradition of our own, evoked and defined in myth, legend, folklore and song, and embodied in the legacy of Druidic culture.

More importantly, she provides practical guidelines for modern students of the ancient mysteries, 'The Western Mystery Tradition,' in Christine Hartley's view, 'is the basis of the Western religious feeling, the foundation of our spiritual life, the matrix of our religious formulae, whither we are aware of it or not. To it we owe the life and force of our spiritual life.'

ISBN 1-870450-24-8

A MODERN MAGICIAN'S HANDBOOK
By Marian Green

This book presents the ancient arts of magic, ritual and practical occult arts as used by modern ceremonial magicians and witches in a way that everyone can master, bringing them into the Age of Aquarius. Drawing on over three decades of practical experience, Marian Green offers a simple approach to the various skills and techniques that are needed to turn an interest into a working knowledge of magic.

Each section offers explanations, guidance and practical exercises in meditation, inner journeying, preparation for ritual, the arts of divination and many more of today's esoteric practices. No student is too young or too old to benefit from the material set out for them in this book, and its simple language may help even experienced magicians and witches understand their arts in greater depth.

ISBN 1-870450-43-4